TOUGH ROADS CREATE TOUGH PEOPLE

- VOL. 3

Anita Duckworth-Bradshaw

authorHOUSE

AuthorHouse™ UK
1663 Liberty Drive
Bloomington, IN 47403 USA
www.authorhouse.co.uk
Phone: UK TFN: 0800 0148641 (Toll Free inside the UK)
*   UK Local: 02036 956322 (+44 20 3695 6322 from outside the UK)*

Published by AuthorHouse 06/15/2021

ISBN: 978-1-6655-8913-0 (sc)
ISBN: 978-1-6655-8914-7 (hc)
ISBN: 978-1-6655-8912-3 (e)

Print information available on the last page.

*Any people depicted in stock imagery provided by Getty Images are models,
and such images are being used for illustrative purposes only.
Certain stock imagery © Getty Images.*

This book is printed on acid-free paper.

DEDICATION

To all the men and women who helped during the pandemic, this book is for you.

To the global leaders who are working to make our world a better place, thank you.

To my co-authors (Larisa B. Miller, Inderjit Singh, Mark Demers, Helen Snape, Jaswinder Challi, Prof. Olga Mroz and Sir prof.dr. MILAN KRAJNC); thank you for your contributions which have made this project a success – much appreciated.

***This book contains both British and American English.
This is to keep the original writing of each contributor***

INTRODUCTION

Tough Roads Create Tough People – Vol.3 is a part series of a seven volumes global book project aimed at showcasing some of the challenges and victories of global leaders. This project will provoke readers to take action towards the achievement of their personal and professional goals.

This book will remind both leaders and aspiring leaders that everyone faces storm on their journey, but what makes the difference is who each obstacle is been overcome. It also reminds us that challenge help to build our mental muscles which makes us more resilient to the storms of life.

"Tough Roads Create Tough People."- Anita Duckworth-Bradshaw

This book is a collective effort of leaders from around the world who beside their successful achievements, decided to share their journey with us and also some helpful tips that could make us become better in our filed of play.

CHAPTER ONE

TOUGH ENOUGH

By: Inderjit Singh

...... *"In my life, I've lived, I've loved, I've lost, I've gained, I've missed, and I've hurt, I've trusted I've made mistakes; but most of all, I've learned" says Inderjit Singh; so, I am now tuff enuff...*

"A Woman of Substance" or "A Complete Man" amongst and around us is not a myth! It is not an illusion! They are ordinary people - evolved, transformed or metamorphized into extraordinary through their courage, determination, beliefs and convictions. They are real persons - like you and me, living in the present-day world. Reading about them, some folks assume they are some made-up persona who lived a few hundred years ago. Why can't each one of us be like one of them? We can and we will - for sure!

Everything we are exposed to and experience in life presents us with a yet another valuable lesson. Not only can we learn from our experiences, but also the experiences of the people we surround ourselves with.

C'est la vie

The expression "C'est la vie" means "such is life". Life would be so much easier if it were all rainbows and sunshine every day. Sadly, that's not reality. Hard times are an inescapable fact of human existence.

Sometimes, life gets so hard that we don't know how we'll possibly manage to stay strong in the face of what's happening, as in present times. From dealing with global crisis such as the current pandemic to personal tragedies; a tough mindset, resilience and perseverance can steer us to be on top of the adversaries. Do not allow the adversaries to hinder you from fulfilling what God has planned for you.

"Life is like a roller coaster, live it, be happy, enjoy life" said Avril Lavigne, the Canadian Author & Musician. It has its ups and downs, but it's your choice to scream or enjoy the ride – or, even better - scream and enjoy. This quote is great because it makes it so easy to visualize what it is saying. Yes, life is indeed like being on a roller coaster. Sometimes you close your eyes and hold on in sheer terror & other times you just have to raise your hands up in the air and enjoy the ride. The experiences we have as we travel through our days and life are what give our lives richness, meaning and purpose. Let's keep moving forward, live life to the fullest – keep growing, keep learning, keep improving!

Tuff Enuff

This song explains what mentally tough people and their minds are made off.

Tuff Enuff is a 1986 studio album by Texas-based blues rock band "The Fabulous Thunderbirds". The single, "Tuff Enuff" was featured in the films Tough Guys, Gung Ho, The Naked Cage, The Money Pit, Ricochet, The Game Plan, and the closing credits of the 1986 film Wise Guys. "Tuff Enuff" remains the band's only Top 40 hit, peaking at No. 10 on the Billboard Hot 100 and helped set the stage for the success of blues-rock superstar Stevie Ray Vaughan and Kim Wilson – the songwriter, lead vocalist and commander of the harmonica.

Tough Minds Make Tough People

The mind is the most powerful tool that humans possess, it can be used to help us attain success or it can take us to the depths of failure.

We ought to learn to use our mind to its optimal level if we want to live life on a new level. We better begin to master our mind or it shall rule us. Once we train our mind and see the positive in every situation, life will be phenomenal.

When the factory of Thomas Edison - the American inventor who has been described as America's greatest inventor of many devices in fields such as electric power generation, mass communication, sound recording, and motion pictures was burned to ashes in 1914, destroying one-of-a-kind prototypes built by him over the years, causing enormous irreparable damage, his response was simple:

"Thank goodness all our mistakes were burned up. Now we can start fresh again".

Edison's reaction is the epitome of mental toughness – not breaking apart but taking cognizance, seeing opportunity and taking corrective action when things look bleak – reminiscent of Phoenix emerging from the ashes.

Muhammad Ali**,** original name Cassius Marcellus Clay, Jr., an American professional boxer with a very robust physique was the first fighter to win the world heavyweight championship on three separate occasions; he successfully defended this title 19 times. Attributing his phenomenal success to mind, and notably, not his physique, he said:

"In the big leagues, everyone has the ability. It always comes down to mind games. Whoever is more mentally strong - wins." - Muhammad Ali.

It's fascinating how mentally tough people set themselves apart from the crowd. Where others see impenetrable barriers, they see challenges to overcome.

Tough-Minded Leadership

Leadership success isn't simply a matter of boosting productivity and achieving profitability in business, but what may bring us the ultimate success–in work and life. It isn't simply a matter of short-term gains but mental strength and ability to take smart calculated risks and rational decisions, self-control, and grit– the power of passion and perseverance in something you believe in when you face obstacles and the tenacity to set meaningful goals and staying focused and seeing through the ultimate achievement in the long term.

Trying to control things – a common weakness in many a Leader takes up a lot of energy. Instead, delegation of responsibilities by accepting the situation and letting go of outcomes, a strong mind can adapt and thrive–even when the going gets tough.

"Don't lower your expectations to meet your performance. Raise your level of performance to meet your expectations." – says Ralph Marston.

He was a professional football player who spent several seasons in the National Football League with the Boston Bulldogs in 1929.

At the "core" of any business is able leadership, growth, progress, prosperity and eventually 'success' and accordingly business leaders, depending on their respective perceptions, normally look for and promote the so called hard-task masters, strong-willed personalities with tough-minded attitudes. But the word success has its own connotations – and varies from person to person, institution to institution and more importantly, to the vision and perception of the business leader at the helm. In doing so, they sometimes miss the mark of creating the success they are after.

They forget that for leadership to work and for business to excel, you need a balance. It takes not only tough-mindedness but also tenderheartedness to make a business succeed and grow. We need the integration of heart and mind to make us whole. Mentally tough people are flexible and are constantly adapting. They know that fear of change, and more importantly the "fear of fear" is paralyzing and is invariably a major threat to their success and happiness. They can sense change that is lurking just around the corner, and they form a plan of action, should these changes occur. When things don't go according to plan, some people complain non-stop; while others accept the fact that disappointments are a part of life and get on with it. They "move-on".

It is my firm belief that we never-ever mistake a tender heart for a weakened mind, and conversely, do not confuse a tough mind for a heartless soul. A tough mind and a tender heart could well be the right combination to leadership and success - and it often is! It is all about a balance of conventional intelligence quotient IQ and emotional intelligence quotient EQ. A great leader partners a tough mind with a tender heart and finds equilibrium in everything - in personal life, in business, and especially, in effective leadership.

I can relate my narrative of a tough mind with a tender heart in the painting created by my esteemed friend and very talented "the wine painter" Judit Nagy L. - a born Slovak who received global recognition as a young talent in the National Art Competition in Slovakia. LNJ is not just a painter and a visual artist, but she is a creative person who moves forward by inspiration. Judit strives to develop her 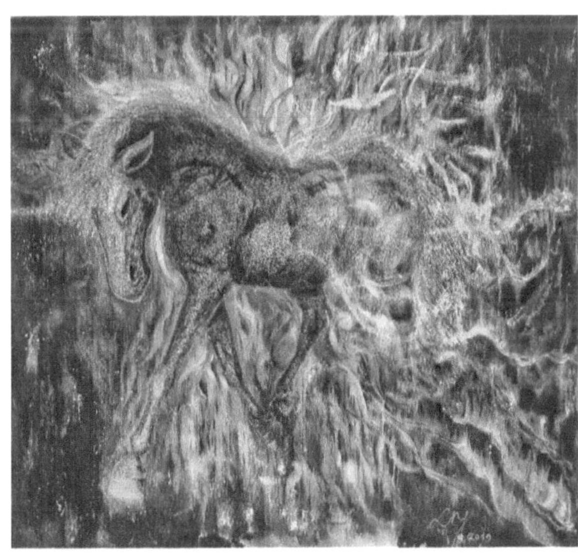 own unique expression with deep sincerity by reflecting the spirit of the place she inhabits and seeking her own destiny.

"Cloud"

In the words of LNJ; "in the movement of this horse I wanted to express tenderness, gentleness, a conscious power without any aggressiveness and modesty, mixed with consciousness - all of these qualities are very outstanding and needed in our turbulent era". She has captured these expressions in this image titled "Cloud". In this write-up, I have thankfully drawn on the works of LNJ to express my thought process; for she knows deeply, that painting, like all creative activities, is "just" one tool that leads to self-expression. Judit knows that in reality we do not 'create', but we are more of a co-worker in the process of creation, which we embody. We draw out what is already present.

Mentally tough people subscribe to Henry Ford's notion that your mentality has a powerful effect on your ability to succeed. This notion isn't just a motivational tool - it's a fact and emphasizes how much attitude determines success or failure.

"Whether you think you can, or think you can't - you're right." -- Henry Ford

Logically, the statement can split into two propositions:

- If you believe you can do a thing, you can.
- If you believe you cannot do a thing, you cannot.

True confidence as opposed to the false confidence people project to mask their insecurities - has a look all its own. Mentally tough people have an upper hand over the doubtful and the skittish because their confidence inspires others and helps them to make things happen.

Never-Say-Die

Never give up. Although the analogy is an obvious one, the phrase dates only from the mid-nineteenth century. Dickens used it in Pickwick Papers (1837), "Never say die - down upon your luck," and numerous writers did after him.

Adventurous human beings, in particular the leaders, and their ever-thinking minds have always looked for inspiration from the natural world – nature, birds, animals, symbols, stories, events, and at times ordinary mundane happenings that trigger their thought processes and inspire them leading to inventions of larger ramifications to humanity at large.

It is their hope, positive thinking and perseverance that everything will improve which have helped to reinforce their thought processes with 'never-say-die' attitude. In ancient times, these symbols were mostly associated with religious concepts, but today they have evolved to become emblems of self-improvement, reinvention, and new beginnings.

This kind of passion is not about intense emotions or infatuation.

The metamorphosis of caterpillar into a butterfly is one such example. *Just when the Caterpillar thought - her life was over - she became a butterfly! Chuang Tzu*

This particular quote comes from the Taoist teacher Chuang Tzu. The simple message has a much deeper meaning than what meets the eye - we instantly imagine. When we are in the cocoon feeling helpless and discouraged, that's when we shake, mumble and grumble, and we find fault in the world around us. Blame someone else for our unhappiness. Mumble and grumble some more and then we are so exhausted we surrender. In that moment we start the process of transformation and become the most amazing butterfly. It is often said, metaphorically, that you have to die to be

"Blue Velvet" born again or that you have to go through difficult situations to come out renewed and grow. Knowing the origins of legends and myths helps us to understand the evolution of thought, but also the essence of the human being. JNL has captured all this and more in this image titled 'Blue Velvet".

The Phoenix is another recurring theme, which shows through a myth that the idea of renewal and reinvention has always been present in the history of humanity. A phoenix is a mythical bird known for rising from its ashes. Accordingly, to ancient legend, the phoenix is a bird that cyclically burns to death and is reborn from its own ashes. For this reason, the phoenix often serves as a symbol of renewal and rebirth. The myth of the Phoenix has a common element: the desire for transformation and overcoming the obstacles. The story of this mythical creature explains that we are all capable of rising from the ashes; then, now and forever in the future!

In many cultures and religions, we find that creation, resurrection and new beginnings are also associated with this mythological creature. According to ancient beliefs, the Phoenix symbolized many things through its different names. The rebirth and a new period of wealth and fertility for the Egyptian culture, immortality and resurrection for the Greco-Romans, breaking with the limitations for the Persians and a symbol of great virtue, grace, power and prosperity for Chinese culture.

In context of these crisis times, we can say that it means growing through adversity and re-emerging. It is a very powerful symbolism that humanity has used as a standard for overcoming and achieving goals, according to the beliefs of each era. Following the Phoenix symbolism, being born again helps us, the human beings, to understand and trust in our potential and capabilities. It helps us to be more creative to become what we want to be. Finally, it forces us to find opportunity to grow in difficulties, to learn more and to be more flexible. In different cultures and beliefs, the myth of the Phoenix has a common element: the desire for transformation and overcoming the obstacles. The story of this mythical creature explains that we are all capable of rising from the ashes. In reality, the meaning of phoenix here is that not all adversity is adversity. It tells us that struggle is part and parcel of life. Learning to accept this fact makes one stronger. What may seem like a 'plight' is not a plight but is a tool that will give you a new life and new meaning.

"The Phoenix's Dance"

Following the Phoenix symbolism, being born again helps us to understand and trust in our potential and capabilities. It helps us to be more creative to become what we want to be. Finally, it forces us to find opportunity to grow, to learn more and to be more flexible.

We often wonder why such a creature of gentle beauty is burdened by death, and especially such a harsh death. Just like the phoenix emerges from its ashes, so can man after devastation and loss. The phoenix gives mankind hope and urges us to fight on. It asks us to keep up the human spirit. JNL has captioned the Phoenix emerging alive from fire in this image as "The Phoenix's Dance".

Common Occurrences or Historical Breakthroughs:

Where others see a common occurrence, leaders see opportunities. An apple falling off the tree, would have probably gone unnoticed, had it not been observed by Sir Isaac Newton - the esteemed mathematician and physicist. Newton's observation caused him to ponder why apples always fall straight to the ground rather than sideways or upward and inspired him to eventually develop his laws of universal gravitation – a driving force, a guide to the efforts of scientists in their study of planetary orbits, and space research.

Similarly, one of the oldest and well-known tales revolves around the famous Greek mathematician, physicist, and astronomer legendary Archimedes' – for his "Eureka!" moment while taking a bath in a tub, when he made a remarkable discovery, what is known as the Archimedes Principle – that led to many inventions and scientific breakthroughs.

Recipe on Tough Minded Leaders:

To do so, one needs to lead with these attributes.

- *Tough-minded on values and tenderhearted in appreciation:*

Great leaders understand that their values are the stamp of their leadership, but they will go out of their way to show appreciation for others; for who they are and what matters to them.

- *Tough-minded about creativity and tenderhearted in imagination:*

Great leaders know that creativity is the essence of innovation, but they must be soft-hearted enough to engage and embrace the imagination of others if they want to fuel innovation.

- *Tough-minded toward vision and tenderhearted in valor:*

Great leaders know to be successful they must have a clear and succinct vision so others know the direction, but they must also encourage acts of courage, flexibility, and boldness to ensure that their vision is successfully achieved.

- *Tough-minded on standards and tenderhearted about purpose:*

Great leaders understand you must not compromise on standards, but they also recognize that each person has their own purpose, and they allow others to express their meaning.

- *Tough-minded on accountability and tenderhearted in admiration:*

Great leaders know they must show results and be responsible, but an important aspect of their success is acknowledging and appreciating those who have helped them secure those results.

My Word:

We have all changed in 2020 - haven't we? We've lived through the most historic times, and it's nearly impossible to experience and live through something of this magnitude without it having an impact. The time-out from regular life forced us to re-examine our values, our careers, our interactions, our relationships and our lives in general, while determining whether we are living a life of design and not one of default. The pandemic turned reality upside down. Suddenly, that daily coffee from our favorite coffee shop or Tuesday boys' night out or those Ladies' Friday social events we thought we could never live without seemed silly irrelevant and casual.

2020 has taught all of us something. I personally realized that:

- There is so much life out there and it is up to us to find what's truly relevant and essential.
- Face to face interaction is just beyond need, it is our expression of existence.
- Finally, we are stronger than we know.

2020 has been a year unlike any we've ever seen or will hopefully see again! It is for us to use these unimaginable circumstances to grow in ways we never have before.

The days that break us are the days that make us too. The troubles and the setbacks are the ultimate learning experiences and we are here to experience life and all it has to offer. When we know what it's like to lose and get shot down, we will appreciate the summit and the spoils of victory all the more as a result.

My strong conviction to share is "The Harder we Fall; the Higher we Bounce".

BIOGRAPHY

Inderjit has served as an airport development and operations consultant in several countries of Asia, South-East Asia, Middle-East, Africa and South America in the planning, design, development and management of airports with leading airport authorities, global organizations and under the aegis of International Civil Aviation Organization (ICAO), a specialized agency in the United Nations (UN) system of organizations. He is thus abreast of the world's best practices in the aviation industry. As former CEO and Chairman of the airport security committee of IGI Airport, New Delhi – the 16th busiest airport in the world (2019) and categorized 'Hypersensitive" from threat perception, he has hands-on experience of all functional aspects of administration and operations of a major international airport. He is a graduate in engineering, an MBA, followed by advanced management at "Henley-the Management College", Oxford shire, UK and aviation management from the University of California, Berkeley, USA. He can be reached on <u>inderjit.singh@aviationanalyst.net</u>

CHAPTER TWO

A VIEW FROM THE SUMMIT

Jaswinder Challi

Sahiba-Nur

**The Journey of a thousand miles starts with
a single step.............. Lau Tzu**

<u>Reflections</u>

I would never have considered myself as tough, but life experience made me a tough cookie. In fact growing up, I used to think that everyone else around me was tough and I would even feel quite jealous of people in their toughness as I wished I could be like them.

There are many episodes of my life that I could be writing about here and how each of those episodes made me tough in surviving. After all, when we are faced with situations our brain is reacting from the reptilian brain and the body goes into the fight/flight/freeze reaction and I've experienced all three of these at different times. It's how our sub-conscious has learnt to protect us in the face of danger.

The one that has helped me to move on is the fight that has allowed me to stay in my truth, despite obstacles and challenges where it would have been easier to stay put. Because after all, change requires responsibility and responsibility requires action which is not always welcomed by others or even yourself.

Right now, sitting here on the mountain peak and looking out across the views, I inhale a deep gratitude to myself for reaching this point, through the lows, through the falls, through the darkness and through sorrows. As I reflect on this past, I feel deep empathy for those that are faced with these challenges currently during our time of covid-19.

This is not to say that I haven't been affected by the pandemic, I have but in a different way. It is said by the elders that we come back round again and again to face deeper truths and that is where I would say I am. I have come round a cycle and experiencing many similar situations on another level.

I want to go back to a time 30 years ago when I was facing my pandemic of life and experiencing much of what is going on right now. I had experienced abuse, extreme poverty, financial hardship, and loss of job, lack of family and community support and almost watching everything gone - a huge upheaval that left me in a heap of rubble to deal with. It's taken me all this time to sift, sort, heal and deal with. I have literally gone through huge soul development transitions and initiations to get to this point.

Pandemic Parallels

What the covid-19 pandemic has been doing is giving me flashbacks of my time then (30 years ago and the cycle to now) in parallel to what is happening now.

For example, back then, it was HIV pandemic that had broken out and everyone was fearful - especially myself as I had people around me who were living a carefree life. I felt vulnerable and at risk. So mirror that to the current virus of social distancing. As much as I would have liked to have pursued a relationship, I can't due to the current restrictions.

Another parallel was being self-employed, and going through a period of no work which left me without money and a back log debt. I did take out the interruption loan which helped, and this reminded me of 30 years back when I was in the same situation of no money and having to take out a huge loan to pay for things.

Then the separation from my mother previously was a mixture of her working full time, and other burdens and difficulties. This time she ends up in hospital and I was not allowed to visit due to covid-19 restrictions. It broke my heart to think that I might never see my mum again. Luckily she did come back and with a blessing - just in time for my birthday.

She gave me birth and life more than once, because I nearly died as a baby and she saved me by taking me to a healer. 30 years ago during my personal pandemic, I was suicidal and she was my strength to fight and carry on because of her words. She said that if I took my life, I would have to come back and do it all again! So I thought; let me just go through the pain now and fight through - and I did.

Also, after losing my cousin to suicide, I really did not want my mother to experience that kind of pain again. This is not to say that I have never felt like it again, of course I have at times, but I've had to fight through, be the warrior and not give into it. I also reminded myself of all the things that my cousin is missing out on, and how I could miss out on even more wonderful and beautiful things that are to come into my life if I take my own life.

I have learnt that life is a gift, it is precious and we should not destroy it and give in to our darkness, but to work with the darkness to find the light. Darkness is an amazing teacher and we learn so much from it. So I continue to find ways to work through my journeys of darkness. My suicidal and self- harm feelings have diminished considerably over the years, especially as I've learnt to love myself more. Learning and growing in love has humbled me towards myself and others with a lot more compassion and empathy.

Being kind to my own self has been a huge lesson; everyone was always so tough on me, so I was hard on myself about everything and beating myself up all the time. It's taken a lot of time, energy and understanding to be soft as soft as petals of a flower that gives a fragrance of love. Instead of being hard like steel that repels in coldness.

I've had to travel many paths up the mountain to get to the summit. However, I persisted, endured the challenges, and carried onwards and upwards like the heroes journey. I can look back on all those paths now, I feel like a heroine who tapped into her hearts secrets and treasures to help her on her life's travels. This is where I also found the doorway to my heart that led me down a path of magic and mystery to find my way home to myself.

I've always believed in the quote by Ghandi, "be the change you want to see in the world". How poignant this is, as I was not one for sitting back and letting the world dictate to me anymore. Yes, it did when I was a child and to a certain point some of my early adulthood. However, once I started to wise up to the world, I knew that the changes I wanted to see would be tough and they certainly have been so.

The Tough Road as a Woman

One of the areas where I've had to really break ground is that of an Asian Woman. I come from a culture that is rich and poor at the same time, I am speaking metaphorically of all things and not just monetary terms. Women are either worshipped or downright degraded and treated as objects. Sons are favoured against daughters and when the girls get married they are expected to remain submissive.

Then you have the societal patriarchal control, to which I've been a huge victim and have felt extremely downtrodden by men in power. This however, is right across the board and I have experienced this from Caucasian groups too. In fact, one holistic centre that I was part of in the past made sure that I did not succeed or do well within their organisation, and they persistently gave power to another female who always tried to copy me and be like me, so in the end I had to leave. So this goes to show the battle against racist behaviours and another area that I've had to battle through in life.

Going back to the Asian community network around me, many

made sure that someone like me from a low caste did not succeed amongst their upper caste powers and circles of power collusions. After all, who was I in their eyes? I was only a single woman with no status, no power, no network and no value - an invisible entity just roaming around. There is extreme power in how someone makes you feel; either to raise your self- worth or to lower it. In both cases, it's a reflection of that person's worth in the first place and not about me or you.

I have been very looked down on; a single parent, not following the norms of traditions and society, or conforming to cultural ideals. A lot was wrong in these situations and I was not prepared to just go with the norm and be a follower, I had to be a follower of my heart and the truth of my light, even if it meant being out casted by the majority so many times. So why should I be concerned about their attitudes and beliefs when they could not be empathic to my needs and circumstances? People can't give you what they haven't got and certainly, the community I come from have not been forthcoming in support of any kind. I had more support from other communities than my own Ravidassia/Sikh communities. Yet, now, I am helping so many people with my gifts from these communities because I have something to give and it's much needed, having been on radio and tv stations talking about therapeutic processes.

<u>The loneliness of a single parent</u>

Cast your mind back to a period of 30 years ago, pre internet and social media. Imagine a woman who was penniless, without support and no one to turn to. A woman who was left to fend for herself and a baby; having to cope with the isolation and loneliness that was suddenly like being on another planet, out of reality, into a void, a deep silence. A place where I heard the echoes of the walls of my house, I heard the sound of my own footsteps on the floor and I began to hear the cries of my inner child. This was the inner child that did not have the nurturing it wanted, it did not feel safe being on its own and it did not know who or where to turn to for help.

As I went through my journey of immense pain and suffering, I also began to open up spiritually. As this inner child had been given knowledge and experiences in this field, and so this had become a gift that would see me through as it was my inner child's sovereign strength. Learning to re-parent and nurture my inner child also gave me better understanding on how to act and behave towards my son - my actual baby. It didn't happen overnight, but it's been a gradual and ongoing journey of learning and restructuring.

Making ends meet was not easy, I would get part time jobs where I could, and as there was no one apart from one friend who baby sat my son in the earlier years, I later used to have to leave him at home on his own which was a painful thing to do. He was like a little grown up man of the house, very responsible and he would work with me and not against me, he was an Angel that was a rock and kept me going, he gave me reasons to keep going and not give up. Believe me it was all so easy to give up many a time, especially in the depth of the loneliness and isolation. At times it would be so deeply painful that I would cry and my son would come out with wise words that gave me the emotional holding I needed. He would say things like 'I'm here with you mum, don't cry...' These comforting words would bring more tears but they would become tears of joy and relief that a little boy was able to have that effect and understanding, and yet there was no adult in my life that could reach out to me in that way.

So, the fact that I had to leave him on his own a lot to go to work and earn money, would break my heart that he was so isolated, that he had no siblings to play with and no father to 'hold' him in that masculine energy. All these thoughts and worries about him would give me a feeling of my soul being stabbed and pierced with immense pain and heartache. Why? Why should a child be in this situation without support and help? I had made a promise to myself that when I was not working, I would try and be at home with him as much as I could and I did.

The poverty however, was still severe and money would just about cover bills and I was always in debt. Some of it accrued from my relationship, others were a build-up of bills. So for many years we were without a TV, although I did manage to get him a play station at one point, which was his only source of entertainment for a very long time.

<u>Working out of Poverty with Resilience</u>

I don't think many people would understand the level of poverty that we experienced. Food was always scarce and I would live on lentils as they provided all round nourishment. I remember having the same clothes for many years until I started full time work, and even then it was trying to make do for the job.

Born in India, my parent's experienced extreme poverty and hardship until we came to England. Growing up, I was always aware of how little we had in material richness compared to many people around me - especially my English friends. I was even more surprised to find myself in severe poverty as a single parent, which was a tough and trying time. But let me tell you how much resilience this has taught me.

I learnt how to become resourceful and juggled to make ends meet. I learnt to rely on my own judgements and decisions, and I learnt to pull out strength even in times and moments when I thought that none was there. I began to think differently about my life and believed that I was in a position to create a different future for myself and my son. I was tapping into inner strengths that I did not even know I had, and I was also learning more and more about my inner power. I knew that if I found means and ways of understanding each moment, I could ride it out.

Sometimes a lot of patience was needed, both with myself and my circumstances, and I learnt to step into that patience through mindful awareness and compassion. Compassion and kindness was not something I was used to for myself, because no one around me had really shown me much of this apart from glimpses from my mother.

One of the things that I had to keep reminding myself was that I was going to survive all this no matter what. Whether the valleys took me to my lowest point or the darkness bared no light, I would fight and push through and survive. So in order for me to continue surviving I had to keep a hold of that belief. In the days, when I had no food, I had to believe that soon there would be food. In the days that I had to wear the same clothes for years, I had to believe that one day I would have a wardrobe with choices. This belief was supported by my mother who kept telling me that nothing stays the same; days, seasons and decades will eventually have a turnaround and I believed her and took this on board. It also gave me patience that I didn't have to have it all yesterday or today, but I may receive it tomorrow.

After all, my mother was the daughter of a wise man and a lot of her wise nuggets would make sense. I also began to tap into my higher self and higher powers for support, especially her father, a healer and knowing his spirit was around, there was a belief and trust in the higher powers that I would be looked after and this gave me safety and comfort.

This journey of resilience and seeking the deeper meaning also took me down the path of service and support to others, just as my grandfather had done. I became a therapist and worked with poverty in many related fields.

Wounded Healer in Service

Here I was deeply hurting and wounded, bearing the scars of my misfortunes and yet my heart was unfolding and yearning to help others. I trained as a counsellor and did reiki healing, and I was doing placements within charities, helping and serving healing. I would listen to the pain of others in their wounded state, reflecting and mirroring to me my own wounds from trauma through adversities. One thing was for sure, because through my clients, I was learning so much more about myself in the process of mirroring.

Henri Nouwen states that an analyst is compelled to treat patients because the analyst is himself "wounded". This concept also has origins in Greek Mythology of Chiron, the wounded healer. We have this placement of Chiron in our birth charts, and I learnt this as I had also taken up learning astrology to help me find the deeper meaning of the pain I was experiencing in my life.

So from my journey and experience, I believe that this is an initiation process and can take months to years, even decades in the process. I found that for me the process itself was giving a kind of 'dissolving' of the pain for both the client and the therapist. Both are working on something very real and deep.

This reminds me of my grandma (Shanti Kaur). When women would get together and talk, perhaps there had been bereavement or some other tragedy, she would say "we are temporarily soothing each other in brief encounters..." And my mother would often quote; "dukiya sab sansar" from Guru Nanak, meaning that we are all hurt and in pain.

Another saying that I often heard her say was "the world (duniya) is here at a festival (mela), filled with desires and hopes, and yet who knows when the life force (prana) will leave and take it all away. What's important is how we touch each other while we are here".

And one such person who was the life and soul for his family was my ex- father in-law (the late Darshan Kumar). He was a person who had a wonderful blooming auric presence and really made the environment feel like a festival, sadly his life force left too soon, just as I was transitioning to a single parent, he transitioned to the spirit world - may his soul forever rest in peace. This however, added to the grief that I was already entering into in my life and it was immense grief that many of my clients were experiencing too. I spent many a time listening to Ted Jakes' compilation from the Potters House, words of aloneness, and sadness that touched my soul. One track that would say; "when I looked around for friends...none was there..." it would pierce through me like lighting and crack into my being. A soul awakening was occurring and old parts of me were just falling away. At the time these experiences were like the end of the world, now looking at them from the summit, I can see the purpose t that the pain was for and how it transformed me.

After this journey, I began to move into more leadership roles and helping others in their journey of the wounded healer, as I supervised and mentored from my knowledge and experience.

The Hero

Where there's been good, it can turn to bad, and where there's been bad, it can turn to good. When we come out of the maze and get to the end, we can say that we have done the Hero's journey. This reminds me of Joseph Campbell and his work around this concept. I can certainly say that from the summit the view feels good, I feel like a hero who has endured the climb up the mountain and I have earned the view that I can see and what a beautiful view it is. I see vast richness with all the experiences of challenges and difficulties, but also joy's and celebrations. They say that the eyes are the windows to the soul and my eyes are seeing the mirror and reflection of my soul indeed, and I thought this quote from Michael Jackson is fabulous; "If you enter this world knowing you are loved and you leave this world knowing the same, then everything that happens in between can be dealt with".

It has been a long journey and sitting at the summit looking out across the views, I can sigh with relief for reaching here and being able to really feel the Buddha in me (Budi means wisdom).

My Purpose for writing this Chapter

The material included in this chapter was to highlight difficulties and getting through them. It is also to show that the warrior spirit who continues fighting will get to the summit one day, and will be able to look back at the view. We all have that warrior spirit within us and it's tapping into it and believing it that will aid us all the way. Here I can remind you of people like Rumi, Nelson Mandela, Ram & Sita, Tina Turner, Louise Hay, Kamala Harris, Baba Farid, Nooran sisters, Guru Ravidass/Nanak, Ghandi and Jesus. These are just a handful of people that I took inspiration from to become a warrior queen. However, there are many more and you too can find those people that you can look up to and model their excellence in the fighting spirit to keep breaking through the obstacles and difficulties. Even though we may feel like we are alone, we are not really as there are ancestors and higher powers that are constantly working behind the scenes with us and for us, all we have to do is honour and acknowledge them, which is what I did.

So, I'm hoping that my life's journey and what I've written in here can be of some help and guidance for you, whether it be small or big, as long as there is something and along with that I send you loving, healing light from my heart. Being at the summit with views to see is definitely victory! You too can do it! Jai Ho! (Victory)

DEDICATION

I would like you to know that this chapter would not be complete if I did not dedicate it to my son who came into my life at the start of climbing this mountain. He was with me for the whole duration till I got to the peak. He has his own mountain to climb now and I pray that just like he appeared for me holding a light in my darkness that someone will be there for him too.

"Shaun, my darling son, you are and have been an angelic light in my life, maybe it was a soul contract of some sort. I would like to take this opportunity for you to know, that I too will always be there for you, no matter what. I love you and always will. You gave me strength when I was weak, you held the light in the darkness, you moved me forward when I felt I couldn't and you gave me comfort in my loneliness.

The spirit of your grandfather (baba) is forever with you and the love of Jesus will never leave you. Your Bibi and Nana and Grandma will always have you in their hearts, you cousin brothers (Ashley and Kamran) will always stand with you.

May you always be blessed.

Much love always – Your Mum.

BIO

Jaswinder Challi (MHS – Fellow) is the granddaughter of the late Yogic Sadhu and Sufi Master: Bhagat Charan Dass Baba and his wife : Infertility Yoga Therapist: Shanti Kaur.

When Jaswinder had her spiritual awakening and calling, she too followed in her path of healing and helping in service to humanity. She won an award in her early 20's for Cultural Integration from Maharish Mahesh Yogi at Mentmore Towers, centre of Yoga and Meditation.

She is now a psychotherapist, yoga teacher, hypnotherapy teacher and a published author.

Due to her grandfather's legacy, she was very influenced by her ancestral roots to follow the more spiritual route and hence calls herself a psycho-spiritual therapist, coach and shaman. She now has a growing passion for writing and this is her fourth co-author book. Jaswinder would like to put a lot of the experiences in writing to help others.

She is also working with coaching packages such as "The Authenticated Voice" and "Immersive Oneness". Both are born out of her own life experiences and challenges.

"From my life experiences, I have come to the conclusion that everything we experience is our part of the journey for ultimate soul growth and evolution, a trigger for awakening, and yes, the interaction with others will determine their part of accountability in their own Akashic Records or the Book of Life" Jaswinder Challi

She has a wealth of experience in working with different clientele groups and issues, such as mental health, abuse, trauma, chronic illness, pain management, habits and addictions.

Jaswinder is also a very active Yoga Teacher where she teaches at gyms locally and a 50+ charity. She is combining her yoga knowledge into the more psychotherapeutic route to support her clients.

Please check out her links:

www.jaz-nur.com

www.facebook/jaswinderchalli.com

www.instagram/jazaro_transpersonal_akash_.com

www.linkedin/jaswinderchalli.com

www.youtube/jaswinderchalli.com

CHAPTER THREE

PATH TO THE SUN...

By OLGA MROZ

"Sometimes you meet people who always inspire you in your pathways, who become more than friends – they become companions of your life..."

Sir Manuel Freire-Garabal y Nunez

DEDICATED TO

My deceased husband (Michael Mroz) with whom I was very happy.

- My beloved mother (Lidia) and daughter (Natalia) and the whole family whom I love endlessly.
- My dear and significant friend (H.E. Professor Sir Manuel Freire-Garabal y Nunez) who made my life richer and fuller.
- My dearest and closest friend (Rudoba El Semman), who is always by my side. And all those who accompanied me on this difficult path.

INTRODUCTION

"Yes, I'm special, I'm successful" - I whisper, trying to calm myself down. I'm worried. I have a happy day, sunny day. Today is my birthday, which I celebrate with the guests who came to the opening of my first solo exhibition.

This exhibition required me to have creative courage, overcoming my own doubts and fears. The main thing in such moments is to continue to believe in yourself, since these paintings are painted not only with a brush, but also by heart.

"The Path to the Sun" is what I called my exhibition. It is the memory of my history, my journey through fears, doubts, disappointments and failures to success, to joy and harmony in my life. I look at my works hanging inside the frames on the walls; I look at these ..."sun"...

BEFORE I WAS BORN

It was the end of January, there was snow on the knee-deep in snow, and the thermometer was showing -38 C...

I was born in a Siberian town. My mother, having finished medical courses in Moscow, came here in the fifties. She worked with political prisoners who, coming from the war, were captured in Siberian prisons and considered traitors.

There she met her future husband and my dad, who spent 10 years as a political prisoner in prison. He was rehabilitated after his death. Dad was considered a traitor and spy, because, once in German captivity, managed to escape and return to Russia. Years spent behind bars broke him. He stopped being a fighter, and made peace with his situation. His eyes were always sad.

That couldn't be said about my mom. She was a small, thin girl, her eyes were always glowing, radiating joy and extraordinary warmth. Dad couldn't resist her beautiful, slightly slanting eyes. Immediately after his release, he began to take actively care of my mother, giving her every night field daisies.

Once, dancing under orchestral brass music, he proposed to my mother to marry him. When they got married, they rented a small room from an old grandmother.

My mother, carrying me under her heart, sang to me in a beautiful, slightly trembling voice, folk songs and drew children's pictures - a cheerful, smiling sun with people dancing on it. These pictures on scraps of paper were stored for a long time in a drawer of the old dresser, opening of which was occurring squeaky notes. Over time, during frequent movements the dresser fell apart and it was thrown away. Along with him disappeared my mother's pictures, which I already reproduced in adulthood on the canvas.

The first seconds of my life, I didn't cry, like newborns usually do. I looked at the dimly burning light bulb while smiling. The doctors shook me and clapped on the tiny ass, being in a panic because of my silence. But only my beloved mother was calm, while admiring and being proud of me. She whispered, "Stop, please stop, my daughter is special, she doesn't like to cry, she likes to smile."

IMPACT OF WAR...

I was two years old, when my sister was born. My parents decided to move from Siberia to a warmer region of Russia. The cold and harsh climate had a negative impact on dad's health. The fragments of grenades and bullets that sat firmly in his legs made it difficult for him to find a suitable job. And who needs an ex-prisoner?

At that time, the region of Siberia consisted mainly of former political prisoners, who had returned from the war, German prisoners of war, as well as deported Germans of the Volga region. The mass of these people turned out to be of no use to anyone.

Dad was shattered by the bitter truth about his lost years in prison after he risked his life in the war. He became gloomy, unsociable and delved into writing a memoir about the war and time spent in the prison.

He often sat in the kitchen and writing in his notebook, on the brown sheets of paper. Dad once again relieved the moments of what happened to him and the whole country in the records. And my mother at that time was cooking corn porridge for dinner.

CHILDHOOD IN COMMUNAL FLAT

So, we moved to the autonomous region of the Germans Volga. My dad got a job as a bricklayer at the construction of the Power Plant Station, while my mother worked as a kindergarten teacher at night, and during the day she was took care of our upbringing. There came out a little brother in the family as well.

Our family lived in a one bedroom apartment with its own toilet - that was considered luxury in those days. At that time, almost all apartments were communal for two or three families, which was a future of the country. Our apartment was furnished very modestly.

In the apartment was a shabby buffet filled with dishes and all sorts of things. On the bed with a metal mesh (dad's cloak and sleeping bag of military) instead of the mattress. My sister and I slept on a makeshift sofa mounted by my dad, and a newborn brother in a metal bathtub that stood on two chairs in the center of the room. Before going to bed, my mother bathed us in this bathtub. In the summer in warm weather, the bathtub stood on the green lawn in the front of the house. My little sister and I were happy to splash in it.

FIRST RESPONSIBILITY WITH LOVE

I was already 6 years old, I felt like an adult responsible for my brother and sister. My parents used to call me Olyusha. But when my sister and I sang loudly and our little brother squealed with pleasure, Dad was not happy. He was afraid that the neighbors would come and resent. Then he would call me by my name (Olga). It was a punishment for me. When I hear the sound of O, and the strict tone in his voice we would stop all noisy games.

I often put my younger sister and brother on the couch and was told them fairytales, while portraying all the characters. Even my mother and father were happy to watch my theatrical performances on such evenings. Dad was making comments: "Olyusha is a future artist."

I did not understand his expression about future, since I was playing at that time. Then, my mother explained to me that in order to be a real artist, you need to be able to read, write and study well in the school. For me it became a motto in my childhood and later during my whole school life. Olga, Olyusha is an ancient Greek name meaning "holy, light and sunny."

READHEAD, FRECKLES, BUT SPECIAL

I was redhead; my whole face was covered with freckles. As a child, I suffered a lot from these points on my face. Neighbours would laugh at me and tease me. It seemed to me that freckles would disappear if I wash my face often with milk. While crying, I would rub my face with the whole of my power. Noticing this, my mother would hug me and stroke the freckled cheeks. "It's a sun spray, because the sun loves you my little girl and it makes you special." She calmed down. Yes, I've known since then, that I am special.

And when, I was teased by the boys, I would smile joyfully with cunning on my lips and hiding my mother sunny secret. I became proud that the sun loves me and in all the children's pictures, I painted men and animals being with freckles - giving them the love of the sun.

FIRST EXHIBITION AND DISAPOINTMENT

I was five years old when I organized my first exhibition of paintings in the entrance of our house. It was dedicated to the birth of my little brother. We were waiting for my mother to arrive from the hospital with her newborn during the exhibition. Our apartment was on the 3rd floor, and I came up with the idea to tie my drawings with threads to the railings of the stairs.

The most beautiful picture was a smiling sun with freckles cheeks and big rays, similar to my mother's curls. My sister was helped me to hang my drawings, as well as throwing them down the stairs. For a long time the leaflets swirled like butterflies and fell, and she was clapped delightedly with her hands. But, as soon as my mother and little brother appeared, everyone began to congratulate her and my Dad.

My drawings went unheeded. I was hurt to tears. I silently collected my leaflets and locked myself in the bathroom. It was my first disappointment. At that time, I did not know and understand what to do in such a situation of unfulfilled expectations.

The next day, the whole family put my drawings on the floor, my neighbouring girlfriends came and we danced and had fun. The world was in the perfect order. Thanks to the support of my mother, I gradually realized that one should not stop acting towards the direction of the intended goal. And one should not fall into despair, but look for the best way out of every situation.

INSPIRATION & ENCOURAGEMENT

Our Parents paid lots of attention and were always by our side, when their help was needed to solve our childish problems. Dad was a well- educated and intelligent man.

He himself came from a noble St. Petersburg's family of former "class enemies of the people." From early childhood he instilled in me love for reading. I loved playing school with my mother. My mother was my teacher, and I was her student. She praised me: "What a wonderful student our Olyusha." It gave me an incentive. I was looking forward to ending up my class lessons to run home and play at home school. Even my father took part in our game, he was told me stories about distant countries.

SCHOOL PRODUCER/SCREENWRITER

I was bored at school and making speech at student meetings, offering all sorts of extra classes. But only few people supported me.

I began to compose different scripts and stories at home to draw interest of my classmates. So, I became a school producer and screenwriter.

During the breaks between classes, I drew sketches where we would pick up costumes at home. I had uniform at school and I didn't like it. I didn't like the fact that all kids were dressed the same.

As a child, I watched with curiosity as my mother would re-sew her old dresses for me and my sister. And in the fourth grade, I made a white school apron out of an old window curtain. In braids, instead of the large bows, I tied shoe laces.

I stood out. I was proud, because I was special. At the same time, this "Specialty" required lots of discipline from me.

I also prepared for the lessons thoroughly - I could not allow myself not be able to answer the teacher's questions. I was a great student. At home, I showed my school grade book to my younger sister and brother, which encouraged them to study well too. I also helped them to do their homework.

I gained the authority of the girls and the boys as well at the school after organizing a solo exhibition of my paintings in the school's hallway, when I was in the sixth grade. I had a big circle of friends, and I was the Soul of the company of friends.

At that time I was already playing the accordion and established a school band. However, I still had problems at school because I was left-handed.

In the 1960s, this was not accordance with the teachers' standards, the common grey mass was welcomed, but each individual was suppressed in all spheres.

My parents were often called to school. My mother's explanations that I was "Special" were not taken into account. I was often hit on the head with a wooden pointer and forced to write with my right hand. My appearance was also indignant, but my mother supported me in my personality. She taught me to solve any situation not by conflict, but by persuasion and convincing. Subsequently, these qualities helped me in the leadership positions.

The city in which we lived was the cultural center of the Volga region. I went to the drama studio - that's where I met him.

ADULTHOOD, LOVE AND MOTHERHOOD

He was my age. We discussed scenes from excerpts of performances together, read books and went to the cinema. Our friendship grew into romantic childhood love - we were inseparable.

I finished high school with good marks. By that time my father was already the head of the leading construction organization of the city, having received an education in architecture through evening classes of the Polytechnic Institute.

My mother, after graduating from the pedagogical institute, worked as the director of kindergarten. The sixties were years of intensive study for our family. I loved this state of the family, in the new two bedroom apartment with the books and notebooks lying around.

I loved our apartment where my sketches and paintings hung on the walls. When friends came to our house, I enjoyed looking at them as they view my paintings. In my mind, my house has become a museum with visitors. When I turned 18 and preparing to enter the Institute of Architecture to study architecture, because I wanted to follow in my father's footsteps, suddenly an event occurred that turned not only my life, but also the life of our entire family around. After finishing school, my boyfriend and I went to my aunt's place for 10 days in Leningrad (nowadays, called St. Petersburg).

This town blinded us. It had brilliant palaces, monasteries, bridges and white May nights. It was a city of love. After we returned from the trip, it was difficult to come back to our previous daily life and to prepare for the admissions exams at the institute. Already at home during family dinner, I noticed that I was sick, dizzy and have nausea.

It wasn't unnoticed by my mom. She realized that I was expecting a baby. My mother was cried and my dad was sat on the couch looking at the ceiling. My brother and sister didn't understand anything. The next day, my father almost in a weeping voice told my mother, that it was her fault. He believed that, encouraging my individuality had led to such an outcome. He also mentioned bitterly that his dream of father and daughter architects - had collapsed.

NEGLECTION AND SUPPORT

Dad stopped talking to me and looking at me. He ignored me, I was nothing to him. He didn't even call me 'Olga'. There was a crack in my life. My study at the institute was questioned. I was afraid to tell my boyfriend all this. On the other hand, the idea that I would be able to give a new life to a tiny creature allowed me to forget about all the difficulties around me.

Only my mother reassured me: "Be proud of yourself, my Olusha, you will bring a piece of sun to this world." My boyfriend, hearing about the future child, screamed loudly: "I will become dad! I'll be Daddy!" We got married. We didn't have a wedding. And now the train was riding us into our new life. Leningrad was waiting for us. My childhood was over.

FAMILY LIFE

I studied at the architectural institute, my husband worked in the theater. Every night he went to work in the theater and I will stay at home with the child. It was difficult for us to live on one salary of my husband. I moved to the evening school at the institute and started working part-time during the day. Until late at night, I sat with textbooks. Our baby had to be sent to a nursery when she was only 6 months old. After three years of living in Leningrad, my husband went to Moscow, finally getting a role in one of the theaters. He didn't want to miss out on that chance in his life. Our relationship gradually changed to nothing. My dad's aunt was helping me during that time. I accepted any help with gratitude. Sometimes at night, I became a weak and defenseless girl. I would cry and think about my mother at such moments. I was missing her a lot. After graduating from the university, I decided to return to my parents. Under the clatter of train wheels I imagined my first meeting with my relatives. I was worried and didn't know how my dad would accept me and my daughter. Independent life has hardened me. I had the profession of architect and next to me sat my native and beloved baby - my ray of sunshine.

I pressed the doorbell. Dad opened the door. He looked at me and said, "I made a soup. Go eat and feed the baby", and went to his room. We haven't seen each other in six years. He was very old at this time. His eyes remained still sad. My dear mother and I sat together all night. We laughed and cried. We had a lot to tell each other. We were both equal women - two moms. I shared with her about my difficulties over the years, about my daughter, about my sun. My mother lost the sparkle in her eyes, but there was still warmth, which I remembered from childhood. She stroked my face and whispered, "And the sun still loves you." Yes, the sun loved me and even the foundation face powder could not hide my freckles.

I showed my mom my paintings, which I painted on canvas a year ago. They were the same people dancing on the sun - it was my mother's picture. My daughter and I didn't live far from my parents. My brother and sister often visited me and their niece. They had musical evenings while I develop architectural projects. The work brought me a great pleasure, I was proud of myself. I was 26 years old. My daughter went to school. She and my dad became inseparable friends. Sometimes even a spark appeared in his eyes.

EMPOWERMENT

I was developing and also implementing my projects. Soon there was a rise in my career. I was invited to the position of administrative deputy director of the theater. Once I met my ex-husband in this theater. Short memories came up (I was still loving him). But working in the theater caught me. It felt like, I was missing professional knowledge of theatre art. I began to study the science of theater.

Thanks to the support of my family, I was able to study and work. Soon, I became the director of the theater. It was not easy to cooperate with famous producers and directors. I even trained my voice to gain firmness, confidence and clarity in tone. Every day I had to prove the correctness of my decisions. At the same time I faced the problem of inequality between men and women in the society. Increasingly, I have raised this issue at various conferences. From my experience of theatre management, I have tried to prove that women can play a significant role in the economy. After graduating from the institute and remaining the director of the theater, I began to teach and to give lectures in the theatral institute.

At night I wrote articles, and studied the psychology of art at one of the Academy of Fine Arts. I didn't have time for my personal life. I was seeing my daughter rare and rarer because she stayed with my parents more often due to my work. Being afraid of losing her, I began to take my girl with me to work. I had noticed that my daughter was growing up. She was quiet, calm, reasonable and smarter in her age. Thanks to these trips, we became closer again to each other. I was happy to realise the importance of that on time.

There were undergoing ambiguous changes in the economic and political environment in the country. It was time for a change. All this gave me a new impetus. I left the theatre and moved to Moscow with my daughter. New perspectives had opened up for us. I introduced my daughter to my world, to the world of art. We visited museums, galleries, all kinds of exhibitions, as well as artists' workshops. Our days often end up with emotional discussions. My daughter became my friend. At the Modern art gallery that I had opened, she helped me to develop the concept of exhibitions. But it wasn't her world. My daughter chose her own path, the profession of economist. She was interested in numbers and statistics

FRACTURED SOCIETY AND NEW REALITY

During "perestroika", the flow of foreigners to Russia increased and their interest in our art intensified. I was happy to work with the new young talented artists. Also, I was interested in finding myself on the canvas. Like all artists, I was looking for my new style in painting.

I was reflecting the fracture and change of our society in my paintings. We were embarking on a new and an unknown path. My sun on canvas was still far beyond the horizon, but its strong rays were already breaking through the cloudy sky.

I visited my parents a lot. In such days, I enjoyed their care and love for me. I remained a little freckled girl for them. With a pleasure I was observing their long-term love and tender attitude towards each other. Returning home, sitting on a plane, nostalgia captured me and tears turned on my eyes. But I quickly gained my pace like the plane that was taking me away from my parents. I was inspired by a great desire to show the World the revolutionary mood of our country through art.

RENESSAINCE AND HE, MY ONLY ONE...

The desire to meet artists from different countries was great. With the help of friends, I managed to arrange an exhibition of Russian artists abroad. Interest in the exhibition was incredible. Financial freedom appeared. I was running charity auctions. While organizing exhibitions in different cities of Europe, I enjoyed the multinational spirit and freedom of creativity.

In art, both in Russia and in Europe in the 90s, artists opened their new paths. I glowed with happiness, shifting my impressions to canvas and paper.

During the next exhibition in southern Germany, I met my Big

Love. We understood each other, having harmony we complimented each other and loved each other. We were united not only by love, but also by common interests. We traveled a lot. We visited museums and walked hand in hand along the streets of ancient cities unknown to us. I saw the art of the great masters in the original and their brushes on canvas. I learned the art of photography from him and I taught him to paint. I read him poems in Russian language, and he told me the history of his country and helped me to learn German. I quickly integrated into the country that later became my home. I organized exhibitions of paintings, teaming up with one of the local gallerists. We had our own house where we received our friends. My husband carefully prepares for such evenings. He prepares his favorite dishes and was the main person of the evening. We lived on our planet of happiness and love, embraced by the rays of the rising sun. The canvas of my paintings was dominated by yellow. This is a bright, cheerful, embodies energy and movement color, familiar to me since my childhood.

SHORT SUNSHINE

But suddenly and again - it happened suddenly...

Diagnosis: Cancer... My husband became sick... My ground collapsed under my feet... I was confused, I did not know how to react, how to become strong... How do I support him when I was crying myself? Where do I find the right words? Where do I find such a book with the answers? Questions in a mess were spinning in my head. Why him? Why my beloved man? There was no answer. I remembered Mom's words which I heard a lot from her, when I was a kid. She used to say to me; "you are a special one." "Yes, I'm Special, I'm Strong" I whispered to myself on sleepless nights.

Having wiped the tears under my eyes, I entered a new stage of path. It was a tough, ruthless, almost hopeless path. We fought for 10 long difficult years with the deadly disease. Most of the time was devoted to doctor's visits - we were beside each other, even when he was in the hospital. I was next to him day and night. I left my favorite job and was not meeting friends anymore. But I didn't let myself despair. I was his Muse, the Sun and the call to life... In the afternoon I was at my husband's bed. I will play theatrical scenes for him according to my script, waving my hands as I did once in my childhood. He would laugh and one night, I took his hands and drew the sun. But it was a dark sun, with no rays...

... I closed his eyes... He was smiling - He smiled to me like that on our first meeting. The clock stopped. My whole life passed in front of my eyes, as a film in slow motion. My childhood, my youth, maturity... A painting with dancing people in the sun was hanging on the wall. They were calling me for life, to love towards the sun.

I was standing again in front of the canvas of my life with a brush in my hands. I was sketching my future; I was drawing my life - my path to the sun. But I'm special. I'm starting a new count, but not from the scratch. I have had an experience (good luck, success, struggle and disappointments behind my back). Now, I have my dear family beside me and I'm happy. I have my mom, my daughter, and my tiny granddaughter - my big sun is the bright splashes on the face of my tiny granddaughter. "It's freckles - the sun loves her," my old mother said about her great-granddaughter.

CONCLUSION

My dad died unexpectedly while I was taking care of a sick husband. I couldn't say goodbye to him. Mom gave up a lot after Dad's death. My daughter finished her studies and got the profession of an economist. She has wonderful family. I gradually returned to the rhythm of my life.

It's my birthday today. And no matter how old I am, what matters is how I feel. I'm full of energy and optimism. I am gaining my pace, going forward with great steps. I have big plans. I want to do a lot more for the future of our planet. Today I have a special holiday - the opening of my personal exhibition of paintings. This is my result and my motivation to find new roads. I can say out loud, "Yes, I am successful." I do what I love, and I have a beloved family and loyal friends. This is my success.

Each of us has our "Path to the Sun". We go forward, fall, get up, cry and rejoice, lose and find. But every morning the sun's rays call us to live and we start writing another new day of our life...

ABOUT THE AUTHOR

Olga Mroz, Dame of Honour is Professor and Director Open World Program in Al-Khalifa Business School, the Editor and Chief of AKBS Journal.

She is Ambassador "Love and Light for World Peace", speaker in discussions "Gender Empowerment". She is an Art expert, dedicated to managing various Art projects, organising art exhibitions of international artists. She wrote many articles about the expression of art as Freedom experiment and happiness in the culture of art. Olga Mroz was born in Russia and has been living in Germany since 1992. She holds the high school degrees in Architecture, Art and artist Psychology. Teaching the younger generation in our developing world is an important and decisive factor for her. She says that young people are eager for acquiring knowledge and are always keen to learn.

CONTACT DETAILS:

Website: http://akbs.assafdynasty.com
eMail : o.mroz@akbs.assafdynasty.com
Linkedin: Olga Mroz, Dame of Honour
https://www.linkedin.om/in/olga-mroz-dame-of-honour-287 28419b
Instagram: @olga.mroz.56

CHAPTER FOUR

BREAKING FREE OF THE 'GOOD GIRL' CAGE

By: Helen Snape

I sat on the edge of my bed and cried.
'What have I done?!' I asked myself.
'What do I do *NOW?*' I had no clue.

It was late summer and I was sitting in my new home. I had left everything behind (my marriage, my home - everything that was familiar to me). I had left behind my old life and the enormity of this transition was descending on me. I wondered what I wanted to eat and smiled. I had the beautiful realisation that I could go out to the shops and buy what *I* wanted to eat. I was looking forward to re-starting my life on my own terms.

It had been an incredibly hard decision to leave. I experienced so many intense emotions: grief, sadness, anger, guilt. I was *terrified* of being alone.

I still loved my husband, but I knew that our relationship had run its course and I needed to leave. I realised that I had lost myself in the years of never thinking about myself and I was most scared that I wouldn't be able to find *myself* again.

That was many years ago. Fast forward to today and I can honestly say that I am living with a peace and contentment I never thought was possible. I have stopped wearing different masks for different people. I am taking care of myself first which allows me to show up for others from the best of what I can give, rather than eking out the scraps of my emptiness. I am in a healthy relationship, doing work I love and am good at and trusting the universe.

What is it that has changed? What is it that I have learned that I can share with you of my mistakes, my joyous realisations and my challenges? Let me take you on some of my journey of recovery – recovery from what many refer to as the 'disease to please'.

I grew up as many women do, being taught to be polite, not to argue, not to make a fuss and that it is good to put others first. And I took these things to heart. I thought it was selfish to think about myself. I loved helping other people and I felt exquisite discomfort when any attention was given to me, positive or negative.

As a child, I grew up in a comfortable home in England and yet I carried this emptiness and loneliness inside of me. I felt guilty that I felt this way. I couldn't justify those feelings and I would tell myself that I *shouldn't* feel so miserable. And that made me *more* miserable.

Is it any wonder then that I fell in love with the first man who lavished attention on me and made me feel like I deserved it? I ignored his irritable moods and sometimes hurtful comments. I felt that I was being more understanding than other people and he told me how much he appreciated me.

We got married quickly and I took my wedding vows very seriously. I worked tirelessly to make my husband happy - it never worked.

I would try harder and harder and felt that the goal posts kept shifting. Why couldn't I make this man happy? My whole world was centred on what *he* wanted and needed. If he wanted to go somewhere, I would go with him. I never saw my friends and gradually lost touch with them. I never had time for myself and the sad truth is that I didn't know I deserved it. I thought it was selfish to want things for myself.

I thought I was being a good wife! Even if it meant I continued to feel empty inside and utterly miserable. Not that anyone could tell of course. At work I would smile and if anyone asked me how I was, I would say I was fine and quickly turn the conversation back to them. I could hide in plain sight this way.

And then I had a phone call that changed my life. I had a phone call from my mother. She told me that she had some bad news. She had been diagnosed with myeloma, a blood cancer and it was incurable. My world would never be the same again.

Deep grief overcame me at what I knew was to come and something inside of me woke up at that point. A part of me that I wasn't familiar with was getting louder and insisting that I deserved a better life.

It hit me how short life is and how precious life is and what was I doing with mine? I wanted to spend time with my mother, I wanted to do things for myself without worrying what my husband would think and do and I wanted to feel that I wasn't going crazy. I felt I was breaking and I wondered if God was still listening. I admitted to myself and maybe to a God I wasn't sure I believed in or liked that I didn't know how to live life, that it wasn't working for me and that I needed help. I felt that I was about to fall apart.

Sometimes you have to hurtle towards and hit rock bottom before you can be willing to look up to the sky and ask for help to learn how you can stand on your own two feet again. So, I sought help. I found a fantastic therapist who let me spill my emotional torrents, without judgment. He reassured me that I wasn't crazy and gently helped me acknowledge how I was really feeling. He gave me the support I needed as I prepared for and left my marital home behind.

As I said earlier, I didn't know how to live my own life because I had been so other-centred. My world had revolved around my husband. I have had to learn how to live my own life on my own terms.

The first step was learning to turn my attention inwards and begin to notice what brought me joy and laughter, love and light. The only thing that I could think of at first was that I wanted to go *running*. I had always enjoyed running at school. And so that is what I did! Whenever I felt like it, I would slip on a pair of trainers and run through the streets and the park. I didn't care if it was raining or there was a howling wind. Running took me out of my busy thoughts and made me feel both good and tired.

As I have continued my journey, I have been able to identify more of what brings me joy which has led me into meditation, coaching and hula hooping! It is a true gift to yourself to follow what lights you up. When you light yourself up, you give light to others. The second step was learning mindfulness and meditation to take me out of my ever-busy thoughts and a mysterious drive to Do! Do! Do!

I was plagued with a seemingly endless stream of negative thoughts, telling me I should do more, I should be better at *this*, I should not do *that*, I should, I should, I should! Whatever I was doing, it was never *enough*. Add to that a constant semi-conscious worry of what other people thought – family, friends, colleagues, the hairdresser, even the strangers in the street!

What I learned is that I was disconnected from my feelings. I simply had always considered that they weren't as important as how other people felt and so I did my best to ignore them. I would seek to do more and more for other people in the hope that that would make me feel better and when it didn't, I told myself I wasn't trying hard enough! But I had had to admit that hadn't worked for me and I wondered if I could bear to feel my feelings. I had half a lifetime of not properly felt emotions and a lot of them were difficult emotions like fear, sadness, despair and shame and who wants to feel those!

Sitting in your feelings is hard – really hard. But I have learned that connecting with my feelings, brings in a truth and peace that no amount of thinking could achieve.

I have also learned that difficult feelings are temporary. In the same way that joyful moments come and go, painful feelings come and go too, if we let ourselves actually experience them and don't hold onto them. We hold onto them when we create stories around them and try to explain or justify or worry our way around them. Instead we need to drop the stories and deeply feel what we are feeling and then the emotion will be gone. If we don't do this, our emotions can get stored up in our bodies and create longer term problems.

Life is full of moments. Some will be painful, some will be joyful, some boring and others captivating. Know that you are a beautiful being of love and light even in those moments when it doesn't feel like it.

The third step was a huge one for me: developing a loving relationship with myself. It had always been the elephant in the room. I had always felt empty and alone and had turned to other people to fill up that hole with their attention and love. I didn't know any other way. It meant other people had so much power over my life. If they disapproved of something I was doing, I felt crushed.

I even remember going rock climbing with my husband when I was scared of heights because I wanted to make him happy and have his approval and attention.

This, this relationship with *myself*, was key to unpicking my drive to please other people. I had to practise giving the same love and attention that I gave to other people, to *myself*.

What I have learned is that we can re-parent ourselves. We can learn to find the love within us and everywhere around us and discover that the emptiness that we feel inside is a lie. Whilst self-care practices such as taking yourself out for dinner or having a bubble bath are an element of loving yourself, it is everyday practices of letting yourself feel your feelings, of trusting your own instincts, of meeting your needs for rest, food, fun, connection and work that build into a *practice* of self-love.

Loving yourself doesn't happen overnight. As with any relationship, your relationship with yourself needs cultivating. If you put in the time and energy and kindness into your relationship with yourself in the same way that you do with your other relationships, you will find the love and light inside of yourself and it will actually improve your relationships with other people too.

Another step in my journey has been learning all about boundaries. Boundaries are simply what is okay for you and what isn't okay for you. I had never come across boundaries before and as I learned about them, I realised that I had very weak and, in some cases, non-existent boundaries. That meant I wasn't able to take care of myself and I had a very weak sense of self. I would merge too easily with other people and identify with what they felt and needed, instead of focusing on what I might feel or need.

As I develop my relationship with myself, I become more aware of areas of my life where I need boundaries. When I get angry about something, or even just feel uncomfortable about it, that is an indicator that there might be a boundary issue.

I learned that my housemate drinking my orange juice was a violation of my possession boundaries. For time boundaries I realised that I wasn't okay with listening to a friend talk for an hour about her problems and then never having time to listen to me. I learned that whilst another friend may be feeling very upset about a situation, they are her emotions and I don't need to feel them as if they were mine too.

Gradually I began to discover the language for advocating for myself and my boundaries. I was scared at first that asserting my boundaries would damage my relationships and drive people away. The only people that actually got upset about my boundaries were those who wanted to continue to ignore them and so whilst some relationships did end, it moved me towards relationships where boundaries are welcomed and respected.

Boundaries create safety in relationships. And safety fosters greater connection and intimacy. Basically, boundaries rock! So, if this is something unfamiliar to you, I would encourage you to find out more about them.

A lot of my journey has been about breaking free of ingrained patterns of thinking, feeling and behaving. A bit like a computer programme, I had been living my life on autopilot, following a programme of people-pleasing, of being nice and agreeable. And it had led me to burnout, illness and staying in my marriage for far too long.

I have learned how to identify and understand those old patterns and how to choose to live differently. I have started to do things that I would never before have thought possible for me because they seemed too scary!

I began a new romantic relationship with a wonderful, patient man. It is a relationship of safety, trust, love and intimacy. At first, I didn't know if I could trust myself in a relationship and it was incredibly helpful to be able to talk with a safe person, my therapist, to get a reality check on our relationship behaviours and for me to work through fears and feelings that were coming up from my past.

I created a Facebook community for women recovering from

people-pleasing because I know how important it is to connect with people who 'get it' and who can support you when you struggle and cheer you on when you make progress.

I re-focused my coaching practice on helping other women who struggle to say 'No' to build their confidence, boundaries and healthy relationship skills so they too can speak up for themselves, have the best relationships of their lives and take charge of their own lives.

I have since spoken at an international global summit, talked on BBC radio and I have written for national magazines. The part of me that learned people-pleasing is horrified at me *daring* to be seen and heard. Now I know from my self-discovery journey through therapy, group coaching and journaling that that part of me was just trying to protect me and that I don't need to let it stop me from doing what I have been called to do.

I have had to un-learn a lot that I thought I knew about relationships. I thought I needed to be needed in relationships. I thought love wasn't meant to be easy. I thought I was doomed to feeling empty inside. I thought I was responsible for making my husband happy. I thought it was selfish to think about what I needed, let alone what I wanted.

Instead I have learned that the deepest love must start with myself and the emptiness was a lie. That I am filled with light and love – and so are you. That I am worth loving fiercely and I am a whole being, whether I am in a relationship or not and my needs and wants matter. That it is not my job to make anyone else happy. It is my job to find my own happiness. That a loving relationship doesn't have a foundation of needing to be needed, but instead comes from two whole, healthy beings who choose to love and give to each other. That love feels good and peaceful.

I have learned to break free of my good-girl cage.

If I can un-learn half a lifetime of unhelpful beliefs about life, love and relationships, then so can you. And all I have learned about how to cultivate healthy, rewarding relationships you can learn too. You can reclaim your peace and your power.

Today is the start of the rest of your life, where will you begin?

ABOUT HELEN SNAPE

Helen is a trauma-informed Relationship Coach who helps 'good girls' grow their guilt-free 'No' by helping build boundaries, confidence and healthy relationships.

Helen has been coaching for over 10 years both in the workplace and with individuals. She has a degree in Psychology from the University of Warwick and is qualified in transformational coaching, mindfulness, mediation and trauma for coaching.

Published author and powerful speaker, Helen has been interviewed on BBC Radio, for podcasts such as Forties Stories and The Lost Art of Communication and been featured in global publications Powerhouse Global magazine and Happiful magazine.

Helen won the award 'Iconic Women Creating a Better World for All' at the Women's Economic Forum in 2020 for her talk on 'How to handle difficult conversations with confidence'.

Helen works with mind, body and soul, incorporating mindset work, inner child theory, with mindfulness practices and more to help women break free of old people-pleasing patterns, grow their confidence, build healthy boundaries and learn relationship skills so they can have the best relationships and be the leaders of their own lives.

Helen's vision is to lead a million women out of people-pleasing and into their peace and power by 2030.

Helen coaches individuals and runs a group coaching programme on 'How to stop people-pleasing for good.'

You can contact Helen via her website or on social media:

Website: **https://www.helensnape.com**
Facebook: **https://www.facebook.com/HelenSnapeCoaching/**
Instagram: **https://www.instagram.com/helen.snape/**
LinkedIn: **https://www.linkedin.com/in/helensnape/**

CHAPTER FIVE

PREPARING YOUTH FOR THE MOST TRANSFORMATIONAL DECADE IN HISTORY

By: Larisa B. Miller

CEO, Phoenix Global, LLC
Executive Vice President, STP Capital Partners
Executive Director, Global Chamber of Business Leaders

The future of business belongs to our youth. As we see the disruptive environment that the COVID-19 pandemic has thrust on us as business owners, leaders and professionals, we recognize that we must reimagine the forward-face of business and preparing young business leaders is the most important ingredient to a successful future. It has been said that we have done a horrible job of preparing the future for our youth, so we must prepare the youth for our future.

One must wonder if the challenges associated with pivoting and formulating recovery strategies for our businesses directly correlates to the fact that we are married to our legacy business models, unable to easily innovate and adapt. Whereas our youth have been reared in an era of hyper connectivity, social awareness, tolerance and digital transformation which has allowed them to take these cataclysmic business and societal shifts in stride, our youth recognize that we are stakeholders of the planet, mandating sustainability and social inclusiveness, allowing businesses to truly embrace the world as our global marketplace. So, how can the 'old guard' empower our next generation of entrepreneurs, business leaders and professionals to achieve the full measure of their potential, incorporating the disruptive, rapidly progressing technologies with the wisdom and lessons-learned, garnered through years of experience? For the youth, as they prepare to step into life, moving toward a future of decision-making, responsibility and adventure, we have a collective responsibility to share the knowledge, experiences and lessons-learned with them as they assume the role as the change-makers of the future.

That being said, I hope you will indulge me as I write for our youth – the young professional men and women at the dawn of their careers, struggling to find their footing in this unconventional world. After several decades of successes and failures, triumphs and let-downs, good ideas and not-so-good ideas, I offer the perspective and wisdom, which comes after many lessons learned, to hopefully, ease your journey.

BE PRESENT, TOLERANT AND EMPATHETIC

A successful and meaningful life begins by 'being present'. Put down your phone. Look up. SEE the world. Destiny will walk right by those who are too busy taking selfies.

Relationships are the most critical fiber of our lives. The most unexpected friendships, relationships and opportunities will appear when you least expect it, but only if you are paying attention. Listen to people. Hear their words, absorb their wisdom, add your value to them…empathize with their story. Be present in the moment, so as not to miss them.

Be open to differing perspectives, set your ego aside and recognize that you, alone, do not have all the answers. Understand that wisdom only comes after spending a lifetime learning AND listening. When we talk, we hear ourselves. When we listen, we not only hear waterfalls, birds and falling rain, we hear ideas, solutions, stories which will touch us and shape us, and we hear the instructions – and allow our minds to see the direction that life intends for us to follow.

Be tolerant, understanding and helpful to those who need it most. The personal reward that you realize when you put a smile on the face of someone who has no reason to smile is greater than any material or tangible reward you could ever receive. While you must be helpful to others, don't be afraid to ask for help, guidance or mentorship for yourself. Asking for help is the true sign of strength. It means that you are open to ideas, willing to expand your horizons, and admit when you don't have all the answers.

While it is never good to judge a book by its cover, learn to trust your instincts. They rarely steer you wrong. Always treat others with dignity and compassion. Be helpful, not hurtful. You may never know how deeply an unkind word will affect someone. We all have our stories, however happy, inspiring, sad or tragic. Sometimes the greatest gift you can give to someone – the way to potentially change someone's life, is to be empathetic, seeing past the façade, tolerant of their differences and present enough to learn from the roadmap of their journey.

LIFETIME OF EDUCATION

Do not say goodbye to education. Your education is only just beginning. Life never stops teaching, so you should never stop learning. As President John F. Kennedy said, "Leadership and learning are indispensable to one another". To be a great leader, continue to adjust your perspective, refine your skills, enhance your knowledge and recognize that experience, while important, represents the past, but education empowers the future.

Don't be ashamed of – or shun, an education that is not 'traditional' brick and mortar. Too often, we hold college up as the only pathway to success, but in this unconventional world, we must celebrate and appreciate the value of trades and apprenticeship as a key component of the forward momentum of our sustainable development. Because one person's path is not your path, does not mean it is not the right pathway for them. Do not be ashamed of your education – no matter how unconventional. Obscure or mainstream, you have a valuable place in this world and a valuable contribution to make to mankind. And education – even if that learning comes hands-on or from a book rather than a professor, is the most important gift you can give yourself.

BE A SHAPER OF THE FUTURE

The easiest way to predict the future is to create the future. When someone says, "don't reinvent the wheel", say "why not?". It will be the businesses leaders who look for the fractures in industry – or within their own business models, crafting innovative and unique solutions to fill these fractures will determine which businesses that will run ahead of the pack of competitors, being brave enough to reimagine the future of business – reinventing the wheel, if needed. As Henry Heinz, founder of H.J. Heinz Company said, "To do a common thing uncommonly well brings success". This is YOUR world. Shape it… Change it, or someone else will. As Darwin said; "It is not the strongest of the species that survives, nor the most intelligent; it is the one most adaptable to change". The ones who are crazy enough to believe they can change the world are the ones who do.

These are the times when fortunes are made and fortunes are lost. To be the former, you must find ways to differentiate yourselves. Don't be afraid to throw away the "way it's always been done" and write a new way-forward. Recognize the value in the word 'team'. As Phil Jackson said, "The strength of the team is each individual member. The strength of each member is the team." When great minds come together with purpose, commitment and vision, the results can be transformational. As a business owner or leader, trust in the value of your employees, making them stakeholders in your company's future. Delegate responsibility giving your employees the freedom and confidence to develop and refine their skills, and count on the diversity of their perspective when the chips are down, and your company needs to pivot. As leaders, we often get trapped in the cattle chutes of worry, burdened with solving problems without sharing that burden with our team. All your team to help 'hack' apart the problem and brainstorm the solution, and you will have a company that will always be the standard-bearer of your industry or sector. YOU have the power to define the future. Your personal and professional success or failure is not predestined, arbitrary or accidental. You cannot attach blame or pass away the accountability. When adversity becomes a chapter in the handbook of our business, YOU have the power to decide how that chapter is written. It begins by making a commitment to persevere in the face of adversity and the determination to stay the course.

MAKE DECISIONS, TAKE RISKS AND LEARN FROM MISTAKES

With each juncture in life, you will need to make a decision. Be strong in your convictions, even if those convictions are contrary to popular opinion. Do not be afraid to swim against the current. Make your decision, believe in that decision, and follow it through to the end – regardless of the outcome. Do not doubt yourself. YOU are the one person with whom you can have complete trust. Follow your endeavors through to the end – sometimes the end is bitter, and sometimes sweet, but each conclusion you reach will leave you stronger that you were at inception. There will always be people who tell you "it can't be done". Remember, people say you can't because they are afraid you WILL.

Take risks. To quote William Shedd, "A ship is safe in the harbor, but that's not what a ship was built for". Greatness doesn't come from comfort zones. Dream big, work hard, and don't give up. You may have to try 1,000 keys before you can find the one that opens the door, but if you quit, that door will stay shut forever. When you are afraid to take risks, you are settling for life, never reaching your full potential. If it is in your mind, it is worth taking the risk.

Make mistakes. Mistakes are as much a part of life as successes, and they often teach you the largest, most important lessons. Do not be afraid to fail. Failure is one of the necessary stepping-stones of life. Failure is only truly failure if you give up. The speed bumps and disappointments in life are only truly failures if you FAIL to learn from the experiences and persevere in the face of adversity. Learn, decide, risk…and keep going.

Success – regardless of how this is defined for you, will require hard work to get there, but even harder work to stay there. Don't let anyone tell you it's impossible. As Nelson Mandela said, "it always seems impossible until it's done".

What you expect to be…the life plan that you've drawn for yourself…will be as ever-changing as a Dubai street map. Be open to adjusting your route, relishing the unexpected detours that life bestows. These detours will lead you to unimaginable experiences, destinations and people, often missed by those who are too inflexible, fearful or distracted to see these diversions as opportunities.

DREAM

As said by football great, LaVar Arrington, "a dream is life's way of showing you your purpose pointing you toward your destiny, but only if you are brave enough to follow". We all have big dreams – visions that seem impossible or unattainable. As my life can attest, all dreams are possible, but how we achieve these fantastical visualizations depends on the steps we take to execute the way-forward. Conceive your biggest, grandest goal for yourself, but set smaller, achievable milestones and benchmarks along the way so that you can see continued success and remain empowered to persevere. Do not be afraid to edit your dreams. As you grow and mature, so will your hopes, goals and aspirations. The perspective we gain from experience allows us to imagine new possibilities and enhanced degrees of 'success'…

But how do you execute the pathway to your dreams? Establish the vision, create a blueprint, identify the people who can be essential to the execution, and take the very first step forward. To quote Lao Tzu, "the journey of a thousand miles begins with the first step". Take one step, then another, and another, and before you know it, your biggest dream will become your life.

Success begins with a dream, and regardless of how this is defined for you, will require hard work to get there, but even harder work to stay there. Don't let anyone tell you it's impossible. As Nelson Mandela said, "it always seems impossible until it's done".

WHAT WE ACQUIRE VS. WHAT WE EXPERIENCE

Travel. See the world. Prioritize your spending on experiences rather than material possessions. Too often we see 'things' that we HAVE TO HAVE. In ten years, can you remember those things that you were convinced you couldn't live without? Likely not. But the experiences you have….the people, cultures, foods and landmarks, these are the memories that we carry for a lifetime. You will not sit on your front porch at 80 years old thinking about the possessions you acquired, you will be thinking about the experiences you had.

Recognize that people are people, despite differences in race, gender, language, tradition or religion. There are good and bad people – good and bad behaviors – in all countries and cultures. Be respectful. You are the steward of our planet, and you have the power to heal the turmoil that the past generations have created, and this all starts with broadening your horizons. Don't believe everything you were taught to think. Learn first, decide later…and be open to changing your mind. As we gain knowledge, as we mature, and as we view people and places from an objective state of mind, we teach ourselves important lessons… and these lessons will allow us to change our minds from time to time.

The world is full of all the answers you will need. If you are present… if you truly allow yourself to see, hear, touch, taste and experience "the world", you may find the opportunities, answers and solutions which will enhance your goals, hopes and dreams. Appreciate the value in cultural diversity, enjoy the flavors of cuisines foreign to your taste buds, explore the flora and fauna native to far-away lands. It is only by escaping our comfort zones, leaving our familiar spaces, and taking the risk associated with bold exploration that we can adjust our views and counterpoint our deep-rooted beliefs. Experiencing foreign cultures and exploring what is unfamiliar to us will allow us to be open-minded, flexible and present enough to see the gift of opportunity and perspective that the world is so willing to share with us. You DO NOT have to physically travel to experience the majesty of earth and the societies which populate this great orb. The world is now at your fingertips. You can travel to faraway places through books and the Internet. Take the time to get to know people in your community who are from other countries and cultures. As your perspective grows, so too will the scope of your dreams and the potential and capacity to achieve those dreams.

SUSTAINABILITY: Caring for people and our planet

Embrace sustainability as our collective mandate for the future. We did not inherit the planet from the past, we are borrowing it from the future…we are borrowing it from YOU, the youth. We have done a horrible job of preparing the future for you, so we recognize that we have a responsibility to prepare you for our future. Therefore, as we give you the tools on which to build this future, recognize the gift you have in the colorful roadmap of a healthy tomorrow…the United Nations' Sustainable Development Goals. Select one or two of these Goals, as your commitment to "healing tomorrow". You do not have to commit to impacting each goal…you only have to commit your efforts to one goal to make a quantifiable impact on the health of our planet and society. As you impact one goal, the results of which will have an ancillary impact on many others. One person truly can change the lives of millions.

Perhaps the most important goal is 17…Partnerships for the Goals, recognizing that we are stronger together. We have no "Planet B", so we must do all we can to ensure that this planet…OUR planet Earth survives and thrives, otherwise, within the next 10 years, our Earth will go into a period of hospice and we will just be limping it along until the end. Collaboration is essential to each and every goal.

We can only heal our troubled world if we start today. We can only heal our troubled world if we work together. It can no longer be us against each other…it must be us together for a solution.

SELF: Life and Love

Take care of yourself – health, mind and body. It is a complete package. You can't care for others unless you care for yourself first. Just as we have only one planet, you have only one "you". For the first time in history, our longevity is on a downward trend. Don't be sedentary… get up and move. You will be surprised what you see when you simply take a walk. Eat to live, don't live to eat. Recognize that it is okay to be unreachable for a period of time each day. This is important to allowing our brains and our bodies to reset and refocus. You will thank yourself as you age in that you will have more years to experience life, enjoy your families and impact humanity.

Be the example of the person you want your children to become. Always use your manners. Say please, thank you, and don't be afraid to apologize. Be humble and appreciative, acknowledging that you don't have all the answers. Be kind to others, even when you are angry, frustrated or to those who are unkind to you. The simple act of one kindness can change a life…change the world. Endeavor to make a difference to someone who can never repay you. Be patient with the elderly, for someday that will be you. Listen to their stories, for there is wisdom in their age. Open the doors for them and give up your seat so they can sit. Their journey has been long, and they've earned that rest.

Some of the most important people and relationships in your life will appear unexpededly. Be present in the moment, so as not to miss them. Fall in love. To grow old with someone who is your best friend, lover and confidant – who has your back through greatness and failure, is perhaps the greatest gift you will ever receive. Say "I love you" often to those who are dear to you, and never leave an argument unresolved. Tomorrow is not guaranteed, and leaving things unsaid can have an irreversible impact. Know that there will be times when your heart will be broken, or you will have to break a heart. This must and will happen. Rarely will the love in your life be the same at 25 as it will be at 50, and this is okay. To love and be loved is the ultimate measure of a successful life, and too often people lose sight of this until it's too late. Do not choose your friends or partners to please others…chose the people who will be meaningful in your life, who will enhance you, inspire you to level-up as a person, complement your character and who will enable you to pay it forward as a person, citizen, humanitarian AND friend/partner. Forgive. No one is infallible – even these individuals who are closest to you will occasionally disappoint, hurt or let you down. We all have good days and bad days, and we all make mistakes. Apologize AND forgive. Think before you speak. Words can have magical powers to inspire, motivate and heal. But words can also be powerful weapons, doing damage that can never be healed. You cannot take back words once they are uttered, so choose your words wisely, and sometimes, choose silence.

Love is the global common denominator. Love your parents, love your children, and love humanity. When you love, you increase your own health exponentially. And we all need to be loved. When someone loves you, accept that love as a gift. Perfect partners are attracted to one another both physically AND mentally. When you find that person, do not let the flame of passion extinguish. Passion – and love - will blaze at times, and at times smolder, but rarely can it be relit so nurture that fire patiently.

GIVING BACK

Be ethical and altruistic leaders, building a legacy along with a career. Make giving-back and service an integral part of your ethos, weaving it into your business model from the very first day. Creating operational efficiency and generating strong returns are important to the growth and legacy of a business but performing acts of kindness and helping people who can never repay must be a part of your personal growth and legacy. Being great doesn't come from what you have - it comes from what you give.

As Winston Churchill said, "We make a living by what we get, but we make a life by what we give". Give your time, your money, your resources and your love, and the returns you receive on that investment into humanity will be immeasurable.

Finally, you never know how strong you are until being strong is your only option. Do not hold on to the past. Do not be afraid of the future. Enjoy today and learn from it. If you make a mess of today, forgive yourself, and start fresh with the sunrise. Each day is a clean slate. Each path you take will be an adventure, and remember, the greatest surprises and joys will be found on those unexpected detours.

We have no "Planet B", and it can no longer be us against each other…it must be us together for a solution.

Larisa B. Miller
CEO, Phoenix Global, LLC
Executive Vice President, STP Capital Partners
Executive Director, Global Chamber of Business Leaders

Larisa Miller studied Political Science with a minor in Hungarian at Rutgers University in New Brunswick, New Jersey, and Organizational Leadership at Penn State University. She worked for the Commonwealth of Pennsylvania for the Secretary and Deputy Secretary of Agriculture, and later for the Pennsylvania Governor, Tom Ridge, with a focus on public policy. Larisa spent several years working as a personal advisor and head of business development for members of the Royal Family in Abu Dhabi, United Arab Emirates, with focus on investment in sustainable development, technology, energy and agriculture. Additionally, Larisa served as head of the Royal Family's large non-profit foundation, which focused on women, youth, literacy and education. Through her work with this UAE-based foundation, Larisa spent considerable time working with women and children in refugee camps in the Middle East and Africa.

> Recently named:
> - Top 100 People in Finance
>   by The Top 100 Magazine
> - Top 10 Most Influential Friends of Africa
>   by For Business in Africa Magazine
> - 100 Global Women of Excellence
>   by Sovereign Magazine
> - 10 Most Influential Business Leaders of 2020
>   by Exeleon Magazine
> - 2020 Personality of the Year
>   by Powerhouse Global Magazine

Larisa is CEO of Phoenix Global LLC, a global boutique consulting firm headquartered in Miami, Florida, specializing in international municipal and governmental consulting; sustainability and innovation strategies; business development, recovery and acceleration; as well as assisting clients in global market expansion and development. As an investment firm, Phoenix Global is the vehicle to meaningful investment projects both domestically and internationally, matching large-scale investment opportunities with strategic capital partners.

Additionally, Larisa serves as:
- Partner, Complete Athlete with legendary NFL All-Pro linebacker, LaVar Arrington
- Co-Founder & Partner, FiTek, Inc.
- Executive Vice President, STP Capital Partners, LLC (Skopje Technology Park, Skopje, North Macedonia (http://www.stpcapitalpartners.com/)
- Executive Director, Global Chamber of Business Leaders

Larisa is an award-winning international keynote speaker, addressing audiences around the world on subjects such as entrepreneurship and the start-up mindset, business development, multi-sector investment, the importance of the Sustainable Development Goals (SDGs), as well as the empowerment of youth, women and refugees globally.

Larisa sits on several international boards, most notably:
- Board of Directors & Honorary President, Kazakh-Slovenian Business Council (Ljubljana, Slovenia)
- Board of Directors, Visual Farms, Inc. (Denver, Colorado, USA)
- Executive Director, Global Chamber of Business Leaders (Dubai, UAE)
- Advisor, Ansari Group Ltd. (Dubai, United Arab Emirates)
- Board of Directors, Geneva Global Initiative (Geneva, Switzerland)
- Board of Trustees, People to People International (Worldwide Organization headquartered in USA)
- 1st Vice President, and member of the Board of Directors for the National Federation of Business and Professional Women – NFBPWC (USA)
- President, Business and Professional Women International, Miami Chapter (Miami, Florida, USA)
- Board of Directors for Union of Business Ladies (Tbilisi, Georgia)
- Chairman of the Board, Read the Past - Write the Future (Jordan/United States)

Larisa B. Miller,
CEO, Phoenix Global, LLC http://www.phoenixglobal.co/
Mobile USA: +1 910 391 5215
Larisa.miller@phoenixglobal.us

in @LarisaMiller
f @LarisaBMiller
◙ @Larisa_B_Miller

CHAPTER SIX

ESTABLISHING INNER PEACE

Sir prof.dr. MILAN KRAJNC, Psychotherapist

The period of isolation alone will not end so quickly. This means that our life habits will completely change and we will be limited to a few square meters and to certain people.

Perhaps even such a virus is "welcome" in some ways, as the pace of life has become too fast, we simply lost the compass completely, we rampaged at such a speed that we no longer knew who we were or where we were going. But now we are forced to calm down and stop. Even if we used to exercise regularly, our bodies are tired. This fatigue is hidden in our cells.

Therefore, it is important to get enough sleep first and establish a schedule or a new routine. Most importantly, it is important not to "dissolve" but at the same time not to be too hard on ourselves.

This is the perfect time to devote ourselves to exploring who we are and what we want. This is because life after the "crisis" will be completely different. We will become more aware, more aware of ourselves and our needs. Above all, we will begin to appreciate our time.

All we have at birth is given time. And it is up to us how we survive it and who we share it with. And the less time we devote to ourselves, the harder we will feel at all.

It is important that you exclude external information such as bad news at this moment ... and focus on yourself.

It's important to start discovering what you like. And after the crisis is over, you continue with this "habit" when the chances are even greater. You will see that discovering yourself, especially through your eyes, what you like, what you enjoy ... that this is a story without boundaries, so that you will completely focus on yourself, your energy and the outside world will suddenly stop you interested.

How to get started?

After you've gotten some sleep and rest. The soothing and resting period takes about 10 days, but when you say now I have to start doing something, if not, it will get messy. This is a good time to start working on yourself.

You need to take care of your body first. You have to take your body like a machine - A machine that needs to be regularly maintained and energized. We need to discover what our body likes. Not all sports are for everyone. Now that you are restricted in movement, you can do so by learning about stretching exercises and breathing exercises. This will make your body flow, no more energy jams, causing you to feel unwell. At the same time, you can start doing strength exercises, especially your back and abdominal muscles.

Physical fitness is especially important because of mental processes, because changing habits, anxiety, pain ... all these are mental processes and the more we have fitness, the easier it is to transfer or overcome.

Thought processes are processes that take place in the brain and the brain requires enough oxygen and fresh blood for its function, which can only be obtained through exercise. That is why it is important that when we say we will start working on ourselves, we start with the body.

When the crisis is over, we will begin to think more broadly and begin to discover the sports we like. We do not have to be involved in only one sport at all times, how we change, how our needs change.

The most important thing here is to constantly listen to yourself what you like. Do not engage in a particular sport, because it pleases your friends not to be alone; or that you have a bad conscience because someone is running a marathon and you only do dance exercises 2 times a week ... it is important that you like it.

Also with regard to "fuel" for the body, it is important not to listen to others what is healthy. It is important that each individual is what is tasty to him and what his body needs.

The next step is working on yourself because personal growth is a reprieve, or getting to know your intellect. We have to give our brains something else to think about, not something we do all day. So there's nothing wrong with crossword puzzles, video games, art studies ... just that they have something else to think about ... the worst is watching TV, Facebook, twitter ... and other similar social networks. Because then someone else is thinking for us.

The next step is discovering our emotions. Emotions do not mean love, romance, art ... but what entertains us, where we feel good ... so is love, just a reflection of discovering emotions. Emotions are really fun. So we just have to start doing what we like. Well, that doesn't mean we're only doing one thing. But in what we have and must be done, we make it pleasing to us. Don't do things because someone told you that you should do it, do it as you see fit and have fun doing it.

The last step in discovering your personality is to discover your inner peace. Try meditation, prayer, chanting ... The search for inner peace is basically the focus of one thing, so long that you no longer hear what's going on around you.

And if you complete all four of these steps evenly within ten days and do it regularly. It means that you will find the key to your balance or, in other words, to your inner peace. Namely, the inner peace that everyone is looking for all over the world is in us all the time, we just need to establish it. In the order I have described to you, which should not take you more than half an hour a day, you will find inner peace.

However, the time you spend now is first to begin exploring who you are and what you really want. The hardest part is getting started. That is why I do not expect and it is not healthy to start tomorrow. Start with one activity and then slowly add. Rapid change is something of the worst in our lives. Therefore, it can be said that the time of isolation will essentially be the time to prepare for a new, better, more peaceful life following the crisis.

Post-crisis time will in fact be our time, which means that by establishing our inner peace, we will create the conditions for our potential, our diamond, to shine in full light.

Therefore, we take the time to calm ourselves internally and be prepared for the time to come. Namely, the real crisis will only emerge when the health crisis ends. That is why it is important that we now calm ourselves down as much as possible, to know ourselves, to make a band of positive energy around us, so that then opportunities will be "glued" to us, which are in line with our potential for people to come, with to complement each other.

In times of crisis, the worst thing is to accuse others of seeking all-powerful excuses; now it is important to look at yourself and see what we can do most of all, especially on ourselves.

Above all, it's important to start talking to the people you live with. Not to talk about the weather and the crisis. It's about emotions, what you feel when you see something, hear it. You can talk about how certain events remind you of certain colors, sounds ... It's important to start talking about what we really feel, because throughout our lives, we have only been rushing and have completely suppressed our primary emotions. By talking and establishing a balance within ourselves, the primary emotions are reawakened.

That is why it is important to find safety and that healthy self-confidence in ourselves and open ourselves to the world with emotion. We say that we will begin to look with heart.

The most important thing now is to find a balance in all this confusion, and we will be able to do that if we work on the personal variables in the following order:

So the first step is: WORK ABOVE THE BODY (food, exercise)

The central organ of the whole event is our brain. The brain needs enough oxygen and enough fresh blood, because the higher the load, the higher the consumers. And if the body is not sufficiently supplied, it cannot supply the brain with enough high-quality oxygen and blood. In such a case, the brain gives the body information to slow down and we suddenly become tired and lazy... The brain will make sure that it always has enough, even if other organs and body functions suffer.

Personal transformation is an emotionally stressful process, so it is important that the body is strong enough to withstand these efforts.

Second step: INTELLIGENCE

The second quarter is our intellect, so again our brain. Since we spend most of the day dealing with a particular problem or the same types of problems, the brain becomes "unbalanced". They have to be given a counterweight. Therefore it is useful to introduce a brain exercise in the second half of the day, maybe a video game or reading books or learning from a completely different area, solving crosswords and mental challenges - anything but definitely - not television. Occasionally we look at some creative content or notes for current life, but anything else is not recommended.

Step Three: EMOTIONS

In third place are our emotions. I am not talking about love, romance, art... It's really fun. I mean, let's start exploring where we have fun. Above all, let's observe what we enjoy in our daily activities, where we find relaxation and playfulness.

Fourth step: SOUL

In the end, all that remains is our soul - that is really comforting or a retreat where we focus on ourselves. Some consider it a prayer, others a meditation, a third a beer after work, a fourth a walk in nature ...

In short, it is a time when we can be alone and concentrate on our thoughts.

When we start to deal with these four components in parallel, we take a step towards inner peace. If we only deal with one or two components ... we will not get much further, because we will tear off other components. In this way we will go round and round even more, and it will become more and more difficult for us ... To illustrate this with an example: If we only do sports, we will end up running a marathon or even longer (or we will constantly need more effort), but no peace, which we will never achieve.

Over a period of ten days, all activities must be equally satisfied with approximately the same intensity.

"But where do we have time for all this?" one could say. We have time. But in order not to create panic and confusion, it is important that you start making changes and slowly work on yourself, within the framework of what you are already doing. Above all, be aware that you will be slower and more tolerant at the finish line much earlier than when you are looking for shortcuts.

When we experience what we like about all these components, we suddenly start to have fun and focus more and more on ourselves. Suddenly we are no longer interested in the outside world but more in our inner world. So in a way, we form a fence against all the negative influences we have had so far, because we simply no longer see them. So we spontaneously stop dealing with negative things. We only deal with our energy.

With this we set out on the path of inner peace. This peace has to be constantly maintained so that you can enjoy the daily tasks. Eventually, you will not do anything that you do not enjoy doing.

With simple exercises for the most important answers

In order to facilitate the way there, I recommend the following exercise at the beginning. Set three alarms on your phone on the same day at different times. When the alarm goes off, ask yourself: "WHO

AM I?" and "WHAT Do I FEEL? Do not look for answers. Just ask yourself. Repeat this throughout the whole process until you feel your first passion when searching for an activity. The answers to these two questions will come naturally, completely spontaneously and when you least expect them (for at least three weeks, every day). So do not even bother to find them. Let it happen easily and by itself.

With this exercise you will bring back to life feelings that you have actually forgotten and that were suppressed in your early childhood.

At the same time add the following exercise: Meeting with yourself. Ask yourself every morning how you want to feel at the end of the day. If you do not feel like this at the end of the day, meet with yourself. Analyze the whole day in the meeting and you will see what activities prevented you from doing so. This means that these activities are draining energy from you. Start to change or remove them.

In this exercise you will concentrate on one day at a time. Be aware of the beginning and end of the day. This is how you actively start the day and consciously end it. You begin to live separately for each day.

While observing natural phenomena in the laboratory, I have seen that there are always seven phases; when an element changes its structure or the energy receives a higher frequency, a step back is no longer possible. So we can no longer determine the original structure of the material or return the energy with the lower frequency back into the energy. We called this quantum leap in quantum physics.

If we transfer the quantum leap from physics to psychology, then in inner development we call the quantum leap the moment when we notice a profound and final change in feeling and behavior. Then we realize that something has changed forever.

An external observer could actually say that these clients have only made one decision. But the decision making is extremely important for human life. We make 35,000 decisions every day. In order for a quantum leap in physics to occur, seven steps must be taken. The same goes for 7 steps in psychology.

This means that we go through these seven stages 35,000 times a day, and we are not even aware of them.

Occasionally we do not go through any of the seven phases and get stuck in place. Then we have the feeling that we are going in circles, which can take years. A psychotherapist is welcome here who can get us out of this vicious circle.

Therefore, based on all observations and a good knowledge of natural phenomena, I have developed a method that I Sirius Personal Transformation.

THE FIRST THREE PHASES ARE INTENDED FOR ANALYSIS.

But in order to analyze something, we must first put things aside. But this is only the first stage. When we put things aside, we see where we stand and what we need in the first place.

In the second stage we then remove everything that does not belong to us or that we believe no longer belongs to us. In life we feel this as redemption, as relief, we feel that we have experienced enlightenment. In fact, we have only made room to draw new energy. If we do not take quick steps forward at this stage, we will have even heavier burdens than before.

So in the third stage we have to think about what brought us here and what we want, with which we can fill this emptiness now, but it is possible that this emptiness will be enough for us. We must therefore arrange all the other things in such a way that we feel that we are in balance.

But the excitement starts to fade and a feeling of fear starts to develop... We begin to think about how much time, energy, money... we have lost... At the same time, we say where was I looking before? I was blind... and similar regrets.

So we should not stop at phase three, where we finish with the analysis...

IN THE FOURTH PHASE WE SET A NEW GOAL.

Where we want to go next, but based on new feelings and new insights about ourselves, there is still the fear and a guilty conscience that we will betray someone now because we have to move on. That is why intensive physical activity is necessary to supply the body and the brain with enough oxygen to make the whole mental effort easier to manage. Although we are slowly moving into a new path, the energy of the old habits is still very present and pulling us back, so we need to be in good physical shape to be able to beat all these voices.

THE FIFTH PHASE: WE INTENSIVE ENCOUNTER GIVING UP OLD OF HABITS.

Here we usually change society... Almost everything that prevents us from expressing our own will. It depends, of course, on the phase and the area we are in. While we may be able to make a small change, such as quitting smoking, this will release 100 other unconscious congestions. The fifth phase is the most intense, but we already feel relief within ourselves, even if we feel that a storm is raging around us.

- In the sixth phase, we take a new path.

In the sixth phase we say that after every rain the sun is shining and we begin to make our way to the desired sensations. Here the calls from the past are hardly to be heard. So in a way we are already walking a new path.

- Seventh phase - a new way.

In the last phase we introduce the new path almost completely into our whole life, where we no longer feel that we have changed anything, although our surroundings tell us how different we are. We ourselves often do not perceive these changes because we are inside of what is happening and the environment sees a big change. We ourselves feel the changes much earlier, but when we calm down completely in the last phase, we no longer really know what it was all about, even if it was yesterday.

ABOUT THE AUTHOR

Prof. Dr. Milan Krajnc is an academic and university professor at Al-Khalifa Business School and at the European Center for Peace and Development in the field of management. He has been running a private practice in the field of psychotherapy for 15 years.

He has been solving crisis situations in companies and family businesses for 20 years. He has written more than 300 books in the field of leadership and relationships and more than 200 professional and scientific articles. His latest work, entitled "Dynamic Leadership Model", has already been translated into 11 languages, and is still being translated into several more.

Prof. Milan Krajnc has been officially nominated to the Nobel Prize of Economic Sciences 2021 by the European Center for Peace and Development, the University of Peace established by the United Nations, where he is also a full professor of Public Management.

The basis of the nomination is the development of a new business model of management that works on the principle of natural laws, improving efficiency and allowing people to work without stress, manipulation, or exploitation. It stimulates the potential of people. This means that the cucumbers in people develop differently than in the existing system. Because the feelings are different, the needs are also different. And the new needs will also change the different reactions of consumers in the market. This is how the world economy will start to change. Prof. Milan Krajnc has based the whole model on the laws of physics, taking into account the psychological patterns of people.

www.Dynamilogy.ch / www.Library.MK

FROM A COAL MINING TOWN, TO MINING FOR THE NEXT BIG BREAKTHROUGH FROM TECHNOLOGY

by: Mark D. Demers

Let me start out by saying I am humbled and honestly astonished that anyone would even want to hear my story. To me it doesn't seem all that interesting. And I'm no doubt a constant work-in-progress, as any good leader will tell you.

To be successful as a leader, find something you love to do. For me, I followed a career path serendipitously to everything - every job and

MARKeting. After all – my parents named me "Mark" so it was written in the cards for me for my entire life.

The other thing I will say is that if I can be a "tough leader" – anyone can. You will see why I say this and hopefully you can relate.

To be a "Tough Leader", it takes a "Tough Road" but let me be clear – a tough leader doesn't need to be and shouldn't be a PITA (aka "Pain In The @#$") of those they are blessed to lead. We must remember that in some small way – their livelihoods and in essence their lives are in our care for however long we're able to lead them.

By the way I've also learned how to be a good leader from many great examples in my life – personally and professionally, but equally just by being around mediocre leaders. Knowing that if/when I ever became a leader that I would want to model the leaders I loved and respected working for. Never did I want to adopt or exemplify the traits of those horrible leaders – and trust me – they ARE out there so reader/leader BEWARE!

One should always add-value. Me personally – I've never have asked anyone ever to do something that I personally was not willing to do myself.

Tough doesn't mean being unkind to others, mean, disrespectful or a bully.

At the same time a leader without tough traits get walked on. Indeed one of my Mark(eting) mantras is "don't let the monkeys run the zoo."

The way I lead is with trust, commitment, respect, honest, transparent, and empathetic - I'm demanding but fair. Honest.

It takes hard work and a lot of luck. Know that, being a leader is sometimes both thankless and lonely. It takes God's grace and blessings, combined with genuineness, caring, and abundant patience.

The best leaders have a vision and get others to buy-in. But the buy-in is earned. It's earned through the quality of their leadership, the power of their example and their commitment to the business, project, cause or outcome.

A little bit about me. I was born in Harrisburg, Pennsylvania 57-years ago to a loving, lower-middle-class working mother and father, Gail and Richard (Dicky, as his mother and brothers, my uncles called him).

I never knew I was poor because my mother dedicated her life to making sure that our family always had what "we needed" not necessarily what we wanted.

I'm the baby, the youngest of 4 kids, three (3) boys and a sister Debby, the oldest and quite possibly the wisest of us all, even though my brother Scott still acts like he's the one who knows everything. Isn't that what brothers do?

Today, I'm just a humble, passionate, caring, servant-based problem-solving leader and mentor, but let me tell you what has shaped my life, bringing me to where I am today. I'm Mark Demers.

I grew up in a military family – mom <u>and</u> dad. My father served 21 years, retiring as First Sergeant. He took enormous pride in it. My Dad taught me to be strong. He taught me how to work hard. And most importantly, he taught me to never ever quit.

My mother was once Military Wife of the Year before she gave up her dreams to raise us four kids. Talk about being a "leader." The job of a mother is way harder than even that of a top corporate CEO. And to think that some women work and parent at the same time blows my mind.

My Mom taught me to be considerate, loving and giving. She taught me always respectful. And she taught me to love to cook, as well. I believe that the most important lessons we learn, and the attributes we develop and refine ourselves come directly from the example of our parents. With Mother's Day on the way, writing this really struck a chord with me. I'm reminded that so many people around the world don't get to spend Mother's Day with their mother, me included. It's heartbreaking.

Be that as it may…

This pandemic situation, and the way it has kept us all so isolated and disconnected, reminds us how important it is to live in the present, to enjoy what's happening in the NOW. It reminds us all to feel grateful for all the wonderful people we have in our lives. Reach out and connect with family and friends…. even if we can't visit with them face to face. Technology allows us to stay together while staying apart -Especially our Mothers.

Because Mothers make so many sacrifices for us over the years, and put our priorities first without a second thought. And they worked tirelessly to help us live the best life they could.

Mothers have always done more for us than we can ever repay. And they ask for nothing in return. Much like a selfless leader does.

Being the youngest of 4 kids taught me early on in life to be TOUGH. I was always picked on and tormented by my siblings – but we stuck together as a family and fought the world together whenever times got tough and we needed each other.

I grew up in Pennsylvania farm and coal mining country. Because my Dad was military, we moved a lot, even to Berlin Germany when I was 10 years old. Travel has always been in my blood, and throughout my career I, moved whenever and wherever a great opportunity took me.

I wasn't great in school. I worked typically 3-5 jobs all the time growing up - odd jobs cutting grass, delivering newspapers, shoveling driveways and sidewalks, working on farms, pumping gas, painting houses, etc… I also worked each night at United Parcel Service (UPS) from 10pm-3am while in college, and made enough money to buy a car and eventually put myself through college. This was my first taste of "abundance." No one in my family ever went to college.

During my engineering college days, while studying to be an engineer, I tried hard to wreck it by getting in with the wrong crowd. I almost flunked out of school. Faced with the reality of impending failure, I switched from electrical to mechanical engineering and switched friends too. We had fun, we were carefree, but had our ambitions and dreams, and that was our collective focus. I did my engineering in an age, when the Net was something, we played shot a basketball thru not "surfed the world-wide-web." We used landlines to make phone calls, untangling the cord when finished. Don't' even ask…

Eventually I was exposed to computers and CAD/CAM/CAE (computer aided mechanical drawing) and that became my first professional love. I began to have dreams of the future. In college I poured myself into our CAD/CAM system from a company in Boston and eventually got noticed and was offered a job by them to teach companies that bought their software (i.e. 40-year old engineers who drew on drafting tables, learning something new from a 20-year old nerd). Meeting and interacting with a lot of people, traveling, helped me to get to know the world better. It was also the period when I was able to overcome a little shyness. And – more importantly it was my first job that I worked for the first of many executive women bosses I grew to learn from and admire and subsequently model myself after.

I never had to look for a job in my career. I worked hard and jobs eventually found me. Companies would relocate me even. That was bizarre but cool.

Speaking of cool; I now work for the global leader in analytics and artificial intelligence – SAS. I love my job, as usual. I'm blessed to lead a global team of exceptional experts who come from banking, health care, manufacturing, all-industries. Our role is to message, market and help sell analytics to solve industry challenges.

A famous quote of Mark Twain lauded as the 'greatest American humorist of his age' goes, "The two most important days in your life are the day you are born and the day you find out why." This quote isn't that "humorous" but I'm sure you'll agree that it is quite possibly one of the headiest pieces of "wisdom" ever spoken. The first important day i.e. the day of birth is important because without birth your story never begins.

However, some individuals are born and they waste life away without exploring their talents or following their passions. They vanish one day shrouded in regret after living their life carelessly and recklessly – without purpose.

One of the most important things I'll tell you is have a PURPOSE. Intentionality brings intensity, direction, meaning, outcomes, and fulfillment. The quality of your story – the purpose (and regret) will become the words on the pages of your story. Make the most of every day. Don't miss a chance to add words, paragraphs and chapters to your tale. Do not put it off…at the end of your life; this is the end of your story.

My mother and father both have passed. I miss them both and not a single day goes by where I don't think of them. While we live our lives with purpose, filling the story of our life with verbs, nouns and adjectives, we must make the most of our time with our loved ones because this is time we cannot recover. Their role in our story ends, but their legacy in our story lives on.

1985 was one of the toughest years in my personal life – first my eldest brother Ricky died in a tragic car accident on New Year's Eve. Only 6 months later, on Father's Day, my Dad, at the age of just 51, passed away in his sleep.

Losing my father and brother and then my Mom several years later after succumbing to cancer on the United States' holiday, Memorial Day, caused me to truly realize that indeed Life is short, and although we don't know precisely how long each of us is going to live, while we're in the midst of life we have the ability to control the circumstance of our lives and to understand the "WHY" of our existence.

What you do with your life is truly in your hands every single day.

My career accomplishments and journey always made my mother extremely proud. My father sadly never got to see my journey through adulthood. He might not have been all that impressed, given the life he had and the things he saw working in the military, and then in a Coal Mine in Pennsylvania.

The irony is he worked in two dark depths of hell. But I never heard him complain.

My father also taught me character and they are; Hard work, respect and perseverance.

He taught me that no matter what your life is like right now or has been, we must focus on five ideas that will give you guidance to make the best decision for you, your family, and your future.

First, **obstacles don't have to stop you**. Everyone I know, especially leaders, have tough life stories. Get back up off the ground when you get hit but remember what knocked you down and learn from it.

Quite simply, life is an amazing journey. It begins on the day we're born, but it takes time, experience and seasoning to figure it out, why, how, etc.

I remember as I was growing up, my sister had a boyfriend much older than me. He and I would always go to the outdoor street basketball court and he would beat the hell out of me. He never gave me easy shots, making me get up when he knocked me down. Always killing me like

21-5 or something like that. But I learned to love the game. I got better because he made me rise to his level of play. Through Marty's relentless quest for victory I learned to be a winner. In the game of life, commit to perform to the best of your abilities, context, and influences around you.

Second, sometimes it's **more important to LISTEN than TALK** (even if you have something to say). Listen and learn!

Third, **mentor-up. Find leaders around you or seek them out from the digital social sphere. Leaders love to mentor. I was blessed in my career to always have someone to watch, learn, listen, and lead me to the next level - In work and in life.**

If you plan to be a leader and go far – you will need mentors and then it will be your turn. Pay it back. Be prepared to become a mentor. You'll find immense joy in knowing you are helping build the next generation of leaders.

Fourth, know the **difference between giving up and giving in -** knowing when you've had enough. Be patient. Your turn will come. Do the work. There honestly is no easy road to success. I didn't always get the raises and promotions I deserved but I was patient, and, in the end, things always worked out.

Conversely, "If you aren't in over your head, how do you know how tall you are?" T. S. Eliot

Personally, I've always gotten in over my head. And it was in doing so that I stretched and reached new levels I never thought were possible… each career move I made brought with it a whole new set of challenges, many of which were simply overwhelming. In most cases the challenges outstripped my perceived ability to do the job. But trust me – you find a way or make one if you're going to rise to the challenge.

Fifth, sometimes you must **give up** on people, not because you don't care, but because they don't. And if you allow it to consume you – it will. Sounds ruthless I'm sure but you all know that person (family member, friend, colleague or team member). I mean people who are hell bent on ruining theirs and anyone's life around them with their Eeyore in Winnie the Pooh kind of attitude. Eeyore has a long, detachable tail with a pink bow on the end, of which he is very fond, but which he is also prone to losing. Eeyore is a fictional character in the

Winnie-the-Pooh books by A. A. Milne. He is generally characterized as a pessimistic, gloomy, depressed, an hedonic and old grey stuffed donkey who is a friend of the title character, Winnie-the-Pooh.

Every single day I live, breathe and exist on this Earth in this life is the best day of my life - in retrospect. To me, my life is a gift from God, a gift to be used with great care...

Even when I look back, I cannot find a bad day; or indeed a good day - or a worst day or a best day. Not even my parents "dehaant" (the day their souls left this Earth). When I look back, I cannot recall their deaths - Only their lives, their care, love and pure selfless sacrifice for me and my siblings. I simply cannot recall their deaths... Same is the case on the many successes, and indeed failures I have been through. And the many people that I call friends. I can only recall the successes, not the failures.

It has taken me 57 years of life to get to this stage amid myriad pointless worries that have had the potential of wrecking my performance, mood and thought processes. At this stage though, all I can think of is the quote from Oprah who asked, "Are you living your best life?"

Or as only a song-writer singer can do – it was Drake who said YOLO – You Only Live Once.

Silly, huh? Actually – it's true and I'm here to tell you that the opportunity to be whatever and do whatever makes you happen, now in a digital work anywhere world, has never ever been greater. We literally live in a state of over-abundance.

So, if you don't like who you are, what you do or who you do it for – Change it. And I promise you – it will change you.

"Only those who will risk going too far can possibly find out how far one can go." T.S. Eliot

---

Mark Demers leads an expert global team of industry practice directors, industry marketing, principal industry consultants and thought leaders that drive vision and product direction, messaging and support sales for Industry-centered SAS products and solutions. Mark and his team work closely with SAS' customers, sales, Partners, R&D, and technical staff around the world, to position, market and sell SAS solutions for Government, Banking, Insurance, Manufacturing,

Healthcare, Life Sciences, Energy, and Education and Communications sectors using analytics.

SAS is the world leader in analytics. It's internationally recognized for providing an innovative, supportive workplace that blends different backgrounds, experiences, perspectives and cultures from almost 60 countries around the world where all ideas are encouraged, and everyone is respected for their unique contributions and abilities. SAS' employees empower, encourage and inspire women to pursue excellence in STEM and their careers and fulfillment in their personal lives. Employees are encouraged to expand professional networks, showcase thought leaders and attract women to careers in science and technology.

Demers' decades of management experience include executive positions at several public and private companies prior to SAS. Mark serves as Board member for an emerging innovative Company – Visual Farms, audaciously inspired to help strike out world hunger. He holds a Bachelor of Science degree in Mechanical Engineering from Penn State University.

CHAPTER EIGHT

12 WAYS TO NAVIGATE THROUGH TOUGH TIMES

By: Anita Duckworth-Bradshaw

"Life has many ways of testing a person's will, either by having NOTHING happen at all or by having EVERYTHING happen all at once." – Paulo Coelho

Life will challenge you and as such, one most develop the resilience that is way above emotional threshold to navigate through it. Tough times attack you emotionally and physically thereby causing stress, anxiety and sadness. Challenges come in different forms like dealing with loss of a loved one, declining health, unemployment, divorce, tragic accidents, violent crimes etc...

Here are some of the tips;

i.   **MASTERING YOUR MIND**

"Your mind is your powerhouse – protect it." – Anita Duckworth-Bradshaw

Your mind controls your perspective, it informs how you receive and process your interactions with the world around you. Unlike other things you can claim mastery over a period of time. It can be a formidable opponent on your path to becoming a better person. All kinds of negative thoughts pop up when things are not going well, and can have the power to derail you with doubt and fear – if you let it. Mastering your mind is one of the greatest life challenges of all.

Fortunately, there are ways to start the work of mastering your mind. Sit back and concern yourself with something which is a life process. It could be your breathe, heartbeat, sensation of being alive or being out in nature - depending on how sensitive and perspective you are. Slowly, you will see there is a distinction between 'what is' and what you have gathered - they are some keys to creating a space between your mind and body.

ii.   DON'T GIVE THAT POWER TO ANYONE

"You are all that is and nothing less – remember that." – Anita Duckworth-Bradshaw

Life is not about them but it is about you. It is about how you are and not about them. No matter how they are, it is their choice and no matter how you are, it is your choice – this is your way no matter what they do because you have not given that freedom to anybody. Somebody can freak you out, make you angry, make you happy or make you unhappy- these privileges are kept within you.

I remember when my heart first got broken – I was only 19. Having been engaged for a while hopping to be married to the individual someday, but someday never came because he ended up with my supposed maid-of-honour… Life does happen to each one of us, but what makes all the difference is of response to the challenges. I found my gift of writing through my adversity as a newly heart-broken young adult. Later in life I discovered that my purpose was not to settle with that person, I realised that I was more than what took place in my life all those years – I kept my power within me. If you take charge of your mind, then you keep yourself blissful and your life become expression of this blissfulness. There is substantial medical and scientific evidence that when you are feeling very pleasant, joyful and blissful your body and your mind function at its best. So, you need to understand that whatever happens within you is your making, but you may not have absolute control of whatever happens around you.

iii.   DON'T FOCUS ON A WEAKNESS

"Your power can be found amidst some of your weaknesses." – Anita Duckworth-Bradshaw

Sometimes we tend to focus on our weakness, flaws and imperfection rather than to focus on things we are good at. We allow one flaw, one imperfection and one mistake to define and put us down. If we look deep enough, we will discover some amazing things about us. There was a time in my life when I did everything possible to be accepted by some group of people. Even though I did what some of them could not do for me, they didn't see my value. Rather, I was made to feel small by them at every opportunity given. They made me feel as though my life would never get better nor will I be able to afford the luxury of a comfortable living. I smile when I reflect of the journey life has allowed me to travel on, because it amazes me to know that I am still standing despite it all. Although my love and support was seen as a weakness, but I found my strength to move hard on myself so as to become the person that I am today – never give focus on your weakness. Focus on your strength because that is what will announce you to your world and that is your narrative

iv.   DO THESE FIVE THINGS BEFORE SLEEPING

- Eat health meal hours before going to bed
- Take a shower/ hot bath
- Light an organic Oil lamp
- Meditate/ pray
- Remind yourself: " I am not this body, I am not this mind"

If you practice the above mentioned, there is something positive you will notice about yourself.

v.   INTERMITTENT FASTING IS GOOD FOR YOUR HEALTH

Avoid eating much more than you can eat because any correction or creation that needs to happen in your body, the stomach needs to be empty. Health is not something you do from outside but something you do from within. If you have the zeal, do one meal a day for the next 30 days and you will loss a few kilos feeling healthier and more energetic. Fasting is an incredibly powerful health hack that can literally save your life as well as empower your Spiritual life.

vi.   MAKE A DECISION

If you want to set goals for your life or take a decision, it would be good that you take a break from all influences such as family influence, social influence and other influences. Withdraw somewhere, sit down, meditate and bring yourself to a certain level of clarity and joy. When you are very happy, you must decide what is it that you want to become in life and what is it that would be enduring whilst pushing the goals. Do not be in a position of desperation to set goals. Desperate goals may not be enduring as a result of lack of clarity.

vii.   SURVIVAL INSTINCT:

You must find a way to deploy your natural ability to do anything and everything to stay alive - especially when you are in a dangerous situation. Suppose you are about to be attacked by a wild animal; you will either run for safety or be in defense. Likewise, a person who is lost in the forest would find a means to eat and drink water in order to survive before rescue. Achieving this requires a proportional decision that would not jeopardies your set goals.

viii. KEEP PLAN PRIVATE

You don't have to trust that someone is never going to betray you, you have to trust whether you will be able to handle it if they do, and that you will be able to walk away. Stop worrying about whether you can trust someone else or not. It is a pointless waste of your energy to worry about. Worry only about yourself.

People who know you are more dangerous to you than a stranger. People who know you know your weakness, failure, shortcomings and they can use these against you. Strangers are only interested in the value that you bring to the table. People who know you envy you and try to sabotage your progress, success and advancement in life, but strangers receive your value and help you rise in life. Remember, privacy is power because what people do not know, they cannot destroy. Learn to keep your plans private and move in silence.

ix. BUILD QUALITY RELATIONSHIP (Networking)

You need to surround yourself with people of great and like-minds who have wealth of knowledge and experience in your area of endeavour. It is pertinent to walk with wise people and you will be next and the same work the other way. You have to be stingy with your time. Don't waste it on people that are not like-minded, resentment and don't waste it doing things that you know are not part of your dream plan.

x. DON'T COMPARE

You should never compare yourself with someone else otherwise you will remain a captive whose life would be dictated by others who may not know you even exist. It is different from having a mentor you wish to learn and emulate. Rather, you should keep striving to improve in your field of endeavour by carrying out extensive research, read books on successful people in your area of interest for knowledge and experience. You must be competent if you must win in the field of play. Instead of comparing yourself with others, consider paying attention on how to become more competence in your work - focus on enhancing your competence. When you do this, you will see there is such joy in breaking limitations every day and becoming better in what you do. If you are breaking limitations in your field of play, if your competence level is improving and working constantly to expand, you will not bother neither have the time to pay attention to what somebody else is doing.

xi.   Understand your life purpose

"When a purpose is not known, others would determine one's destination." – Anita Duckworth-Bradshaw

You need to know that only in transcendence can there be transformation. When you keep rising from where you are right now, one day you will be profoundly transformed. Transformation does not mean that you try to change the shape that you are, but it means you rise above things that control you and matter to you. When you rise above limited needs, compulsion and longings, you will be transformed. Transformation is not something that you chart. You just chart your journey and awaken the giant within you (freeing your mind, body and spirit). Develop the ability of let go and rise above dark and stormy waters- a journey to the truest self.

xii. BE PLAYFUL

"Life is a dance, because each step you take leads to another and another and..." – Anita Duckworth-Bradshaw

The most responsible way to live is that you are playful with life. It's absolutely irresponsible to carry a long face and walk around in this world in misery. So being playful is not irresponsibility but responsible and responsive to life. Only when you are playful you can pay attention to everything but when you are serious the world does not exist for you. When you are not playful you are totally enslaved by the process of your mind, your thoughts, your opinions, your ideologies, your rights and wrongs, your moralities then only you lost your playfulness. If you are in line with the large creation there is no other way to be, you will be playful. Only if you are playful, you can truly grapple with the problems in the world without being affected by it and do your best about it. If you do not know how to be playful, those problems are capable of eating you up. If you maintain a few hours of playfulness in a day about what you are doing, you will notice that your physical body will start functioning so much better.

xiii. WORDS OF ADVICE

There two things you should never have to chase – True friends and true love. People make time for who they want to make time for. People text and reply to people they want to talk to. When someone tells you that they are too busy continuously, believe them. Don't try to convince them otherwise, don't try to force them to make time for you, if they want to, they will. It hurts but you can't force someone to have feelings for you. You should not have to beg someone to love you...you should not have to beg someone to care...you should not have to beg someone to try...you should not have to beg someone to talk to you and you should not have beg to someone to put you first, if they wanted to, they would. Don't let people become a priority in your life when all you are to them is an option.

xiv. LET GO OF THE NEGATIVITY

First of all, you need to understand your anger, resentment, fear and anxiety are the negativity that you generate. Fortunately, life does not work like that. So, we need to understand that if you are chemically analyzed right now to know your blood work and checked back five minutes later after intense anger, there will be negative element in it and it shows that you are literally are hurting yourself.

References:
https://vm.tiktok.com/ZMeyrBxbj/ Mind Transformation Therapy

hhps://youtube.com/c/sadhguru

ABOUT THE AUTHOR

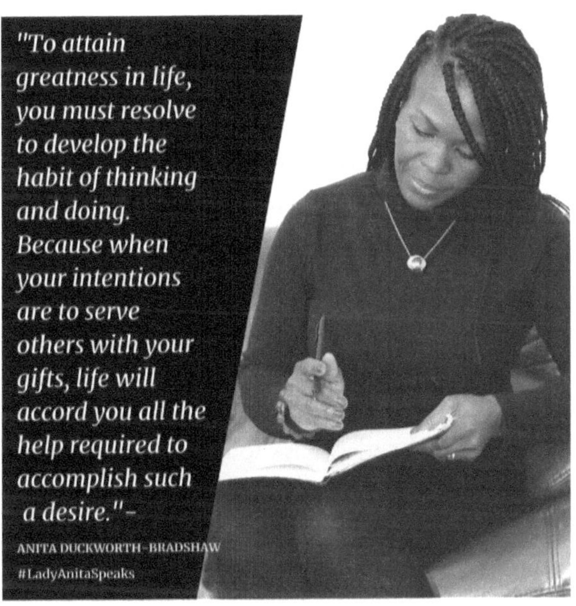

Lady Anita Chioma Duckworth-Bradshaw is an Award winning Global Impact Leader, Best Selling Author, Change Agent, Life Coach, and the Creator of the Powerhouse Global Brand (Powerhouse Global Magazine, Powerhouse Global Awards and Powerhouse Global Conferences).

Her eye for beauty, her talent for design, and her imaginative and creative skills have led her to build a global social media platform that helps further her social work. Culminating in an elegant and most sophisticated publication that serves humanity and shares their stories, she's managed to create a world where to feature women and men alike. Her brilliant use of social media allows her to vastly influence the masses. With a distribution reach of 88 countries of the world Lady Anita helps feed minds and touch souls.

Lady Anita is a true embodiment of a servant leader. She has created a platform for men and women alike from all spheres of life to showcase their brilliance. Through online presence she gives hope to many people – especially women.

Her own personal struggles gave birth to her purpose. Having grown up in Africa, she understands first hand, the importance of supporting others and helping provide ways to have life's basic needs met. She found a solution and therefore, created her foundation Powerful Global Women Foundation (PGWF) in 2016 in Nigeria and subsequently, her most radiant Powerhouse Global Magazine publications .9

It is both Lady Anita's personal and professional mission to assist and serve others. Lady Anita travels the world speaking at conferences and organizing Powerhouse Global events. She lives by her motto of: Transforming Lives - one person at a time. Utilizing her voice, she addresses pressing issues and topics related to her work.

Topics such as: Global Visibility; Your Voice. Your Power; Reposition for change; The Leading Leader; Risk to Reward; Healing From Within; The Road To Discovery and others.

Connect with Lady Anita today.

Twitter - @Laproverbs
LinkedIn - @LadyAnitaDuckworth-Bradshaw
IG: Anita Bradshaw

Web: www.powerhouseglobalstars.com
www.powerhouseglobalwomen.com

www.ingramcontent.com/pod-product-compliance
Lightning Source LLC
Chambersburg PA
CBHW031139250726
48655CB00002B/741